SH*T

WISDOM

I WISH

FOR MY

I KNEW

20-YEAR-OLD SELF

YESTERDAY

LISA MARIE NELSON, PHD

SH*T

WISDOM

I WISH

FOR MY

I KNEW

20-YEAR-OLD SELF

YESTERDAY

This book is dedicated:

To our past selves for their *perseverance and wisdom*.
To our present selves for their *courage*.
To our future selves for their *vision and hope*.

Free Bonus Workbook!

Before you dig into the book, I wanted to let you in on a little secret.

I've created a free, downloadable companion workbook that guides you through each of these fifty-two life lessons so that you can create your own version of *Sh*t I Wish I Knew Yesterday*!

Cool, right? I think so, too!

Head on over to siwiky-book.com/workbook to download your workbook.

I mean, who doesn't like a free gift-with-purchase?

Don't stop there. Share the link with your friends, family, Facebook group, or book club!

This workbook is also a huge *thank you* to my readers and fans for all your support.

We all have a story to tell, and I hope this workbook helps you realize how extraordinary you are!

I can't wait to hear all about you and your life story.

xoxox
Lisa

SH*T I WISH I KNEW YESTERDAY

Wisdom for My 20-Year-Old Self

Capucia

Published by:
Capucia, LLC
211 Pauline Drive #513
York, PA 17402
www.capuciapublishing.com

ISBN: 978-1-945252-76-1
Library of Congress Control Number: 2020900983

Cover: Lisa Nelson and Ranilo Cabo
Layout: Ranilo Cabo
Editor & proofreader: Simon Whaley
Book Midwife: Carrie Jareed

Printed in the United States of America

TABLE OF CONTENTS

PREFACE

I visualized myself as a college sophomore while writing this book. I wrote to her as if I were a time-traveler, whizzing back to her college dorm, laying out all the things I've learned.

Back then, I had just moved to Oregon after spending freshman year at the University of Arizona as a Geology/Oceanography double major. Mid-freshman year, I'd switched from my original major of Archeology because, shockingly enough, they were *not* teaching me how to be Indiana Jones.

Instead of running through dense jungles carrying buried treasure, I was washing pottery shards and learning long, long lists of odd words. This was *way* too low on the excitement scale for me. Where was the dashing in and out of ancient temples? The exotic locations? The whips? Leather jackets? I mean, come on. Sounds pretty awesome, right?

I went back to Oregon to finish my undergrad as a Zoology major, because it seemed like the most badass biology option available. At Oregon State University, I embraced my newfound specialization, learning incredible facts about hundreds of animal species. I memorized Latin names, some of which I still randomly remember.

I loved my Zoology classes and managed to stick with that major for the rest of my undergraduate career. I briefly entertained the thought of becoming a doctor. That is, until I took my MCATs. At the time, I was devastated about not getting into medical school and being able to work for Doctors Without Borders.

Looking back, I know it was the Universe guiding me. I knew I wanted to help people; what I didn't know (but know now!) is that there are so many ways to help others. And not all of them involve wearing a white coat.

The person I was back then was completely convinced she would change the world. She didn't know about the challenges she would face in the coming years and how those speedbumps would slowly erode her belief – my belief – in a boundless, unlimited future.

She didn't know about the cancer, the divorce, the heartache, the struggles.

During those dark moments, I looked back and missed that 20-year-old version of myself. I missed her innocence and her open heart.

While writing this book, I realized that I *am* still that Lisa.

She *is* me, inextricably linked and forever bound.

You may also recognize your past self, dear reader. Both of us, idealistic souls, poised to make our mark in the world, blissfully unaware of what life will throw our way.

I hope these lessons bring clarity, insight, and a few laughs during your journey of self-exploration and awakening. I invite you to explore how your life experiences have prepared you to be right here, right now, reading this book.

I believe that by owning our stories - as I've done throughout this book - and identifying the hard-won lessons in our lives, we *are* changing the world together.

One self-reflection,
One powerful conversation,
One breakthrough,
One moment of vulnerability,
One act of kindness and empathy,
At a time.

xoxox
Lisa

INTRODUCTION

I want to pause and say one thing very clearly: this book is not about *regret*.

I don't regret my journey or past decisions. That doesn't mean I'm not curious about what my life would have been like if I'd had some of these skills and insights earlier in my journey. Perhaps you feel the same way. I choose not to look at my past through a judgmental lens. It is just a series of events. There is nothing good or bad, unless we make it so.

I don't know where you are in your journey. You might be just starting out and curious about the lessons from someone else's life. You might be far along in your exploration, reflecting back on each moment of clarity and wisdom you experienced along the way.

In my view, it doesn't matter where you are along that path, as long as you have started walking.

You'll know you've taken that first step by the uncomfortable, unsettled nature of your days. You'll feel like you're pushing against restraints, like nothing makes you happy, that none of your choices *work out*. That's when you know you're ready to start *your* journey of self-discovery and self-actualization. Buckle up! It's one hell of a ride.

This book is organized into fifty-two *Life Lessons*, conveniently, one for every week of the year. Each lesson delves into an insight that I wanted to pass on to my younger self, to help guide her journey. So, essentially, this book represents a year's worth of self-exploration based on lessons I've learned over the past two decades!

At the end of each *Life Lesson*, I've included a few *Life Lesson Challenges*. I invite you to contemplate these questions as you read each chapter.

Since I'm all about getting the most bang for your buck, here are some ideas on how to fully explore these challenges.

- **Download the free companion workbook at siwiky-book.com!**
- Start a new journal and dedicate an hour each week to answering the questions for yourself.
- Grab some friends and create a weekly or monthly book club.
- Answer the questions out loud and record an audio memo.
- Create a mini video with your favorite background music.
- Share them with your social media network (and tag me so I can celebrate it and you!).

There's no right or wrong way to do this. Trust me. Write notes, highlight sentences, add multi-colored sticky notes. Flip forward or walk through the lessons in order. It's your choice! Enjoy, and see you on the other side.

xoxox

LIFE LESSON 1

I Wish I Knew that My Intuition
is Always Right

This lesson is all about intuition. How does one describe something so indescribable? Merriam-Webster defines intuition as, *"direct knowledge or cognition without evident rational thought and inference."* I've come to think of intuition as a sense of deep *knowing* and conviction. This is especially true if the *knowing* seems completely illogical at first. I use many words to describe intuition: hunch, gut instinct. Listening to my intuition and taking actions guided by intuition have proven to be profound, life-changing decisions. What is your gut telling you about your life?

Dear Lisa,

This is a long story. It's a long story because this is a particularly challenging lesson for you (and many others) to learn: how to trust what your intuition is telling you. You'll face this challenge many times in your young life, but two examples stand out most vividly.

The first time you'll suffer severe life-changing consequences by ignoring your intuition will be late 2004. You'll be in the middle of your doctoral research at the University of North Carolina in Chapel Hill. Your research will often require you to spend twenty-four-hour periods at the lab, counting parasites in samples over the course of the day.

For weeks, you'll push to get data collected in anticipation of a big conference. Another doctoral student and you will be invited to present in front of a European Working Group on tropical parasitic disease, in Antwerp, Belgium. It's a big deal.

This will translate into very long days at the lab, stress, poor diet, and little to no sleep. During those long days, you'll begin to experience very heavy and irregular menstrual periods. And, you'll begin to feel a hardening in your lower abdomen. You'll brush aside those voices inside your head telling you to get this checked out. You'll tell yourself, "*I don't have time to get help.*"

The morning of the flight to Belgium, you'll bring two extra pairs of pants in your carry-on because you'll have bled through your clothes every day for the past week, despite doing everything you could to prevent that.

You arrive in Antwerp for the conference, pale, undoubtedly anemic, sleep-deprived, but also feeling ecstatic. This is your big chance!

The data presentation itself will go very well; you'll receive wonderful accolades from the attendees and your thesis advisors. But again, later that night, at the tiny economy hotel, you'll again bled through your pajamas, soaking the bedsheets.

You'll know *something* is wrong. Your intuition will be clamoring for your attention. This isn't stress or sleep deprivation. The bulge in your lower abdomen keeps growing and growing. You'll have few clothes left that fit.

You'll be so deep in shame from the inability to *control* your body (more on this control thing later), so unwilling to admit *weakness* and see the doctor, that you'll continue working for another three weeks after returning home from Belgium.

Then, one afternoon, you'll be working away in the lab, perched on a tall stool in front of a biohazard hood. And you'll pass out; you won't remember it actually happening. But you'll fall, right off the stool, with tools and samples crashing all around you. A student down the hall will hear the chaos and find you on the floor. A large amount of blood will have soaked through the back of your white lab coat.

She'll help you sit up and try to convince you to visit the Emergency Room. Ironically, your lab is located within the medical school and you can practically see the hospital from your window. Your inner voice will be screaming for you to get help. But still, you'll resist.

You won't know to stop and connect with your intuition. You won't know how to combat those powerful shame tapes running through your head. You won't want to make a fuss or put anyone out. Their feelings and (assumed) judgements about you will seem more important than your health or safety.

For most of your adult life you will have a block around not getting sick, not being lazy, not taking breaks, not showing weakness.

When you finally go see a doctor, he'll tell you a very large tumor is growing in your lower abdomen. After six weeks of testing, a near-fatal pulmonary embolism, and (eventually) exploratory surgery, you'll wake up in a hospital room blessedly tumor-free but without the ability to conceive or bear children.

You won't learn the lesson here – the lesson of listening to your intuition screaming at you that *something is wrong*! You'll continue to ignore your intuition. Your professional career will be marked by short tenures at companies – some for good reasons, some because of fear. You'll talk yourself into a series of new jobs. You'll try to enjoy them. You'll try to rekindle the passion you had for science when you were younger. And all the while, ignoring that deep knowing, that intuition, that something is not right.

At first, you'll blame external things for your angst: the companies, co-workers, job requirements, commute. These *excuses* will become increasingly ludicrous as your unhappiness deepens. At one point, you'll explain your choice to leave a company based on the office décor and quality of silverware in the shared kitchen. No, seriously.

During these years, you'll judge and blame yourself for not being *enough*. You'll find a temporary escape hatch in the form of a virtual consulting role, one that allows you to work nearly 100% from home. It'll sound like heaven. NO commute. NO political maneuvering. NO ugly carpet. NO flimsy spoons.

And, for a few years, the consulting job will be perfect for you. The background chorus of dissatisfaction will still be there; and, as the months march by, it'll start to crescendo just like it has in every other job.

However, this time, you can no longer blame the company's building or location (or décor or spoons) for this increasingly hard-to-ignore dissonance. Instead, all that blame will land squarely on your shoulders.

Now, if you ask your colleagues, you'll discover you do a decent job hiding all of this. That is, until you hit emotional rock-bottom.

Then, there will be no hiding from anyone, least of all yourself.

The is the second time ignoring your intuition nearly costs you everything.

It goes without saying, obviously, that these will be difficult times. It'll feel like you're trudging through wet cement, your head will feel wrapped in layers of cotton gauze. There'll be no light. There'll be no hope. You'll be swimming in the deepest, darkest part of an oceanic abyss.

Maybe swimming isn't the right word. That sounds too active. At best, you'll be treading water. It's fair to say you'll be clinically depressed and, at times, suicidal.

However, you fancy yourself to be *tough*. What does your gut know? I mean, you're a data-driven person; you don't operate on crazy hunches or wimpy thoughts! Your intuition will be tugging at your sleeve, telling you to tell someone how you're feeling, to reach out for help.

Ignoring that deep intuitive *knowing* to reach out for help, to press pause on your life until you can figure out what's happening, means you'll numb out 24/7/365. You'll shove all that inadequacy, self-blame, shaming, and fatigue deep down. You'll numb with work. You'll eat food that doesn't fuel your body, or you won't eat at all. You'll try to exercise the demons away. You'll shop compulsively, trying to fill the abyss with things that are supposed to make you feel whole. You'll overspend and push yourself into multiple financial crises. You'll be arrested.

You'll live in denial of how right your gut *actually* is when it yells at you to get help, that something is wrong, that you're rapidly sliding down a slippery slope to despair.

You will weep when no one is watching. You'll consider cutting yourself, but won't know how to hide it from your partner. You'll have visions of crashing your car into bridge pilings while driving to the grocery store, tears streaming down your face.

And, still you won't get help. You'll think by ignoring and suppressing those intuitive hits, you'll make yourself stronger; what you won't know is that you won't rise to the ocean's surface. Suppressing these emotions will weigh you down, pulling you deeper and deeper into the darkness.

The breaking point will come, as it always does, how and when you'll need it to (more on synchronicity later). You and your partner will be visiting your parents at their new house on the Oregon coast.

You won't take the time off from your consulting job for this trip like your intuition told you – you will be incapable of self-advocating or self-care at this point. One weekday during your visit, you'll find yourself hunched over your laptop on the couch, phone squished against your ear. At this point, the voice inside your head will be screaming for relief.

During that phone call, two of your colleagues will give you routine feedback on a project deliverable. Every word will feel like an actual dagger wound. Your stomach will churn, and you'll feel nauseous. You'll know, just like you knew before, before they found the tumor, that *something* is wrong. That's your intuition. You'll push that feeling away, and get angry on the call, forcing an argument just so you can hang up the phone.

Your mom will be sitting a few feet away on the couch from you, looking at you with concern. You'll glance her way and then bolt downstairs, running for the bathroom, afraid of throwing up all over their new floor.

You'll make it to the bathroom but instead of vomiting, you'll slide down the wall by the toilet and start sobbing convulsively. Your entire body will shake. You'll feel naked, exposed, beaten down, weak, and hopeless. The shame tapes will be playing a full volume in your mind. You'll think, *why am I such a screw-up? Why can't I do anything right? I am so stupid, so worthless. I can't live like this anymore.*

You won't see any options. You won't see a way out of the abyss. The pressure of that deep water is crushing you. Looking back, I know that if you'd trusted your gut as I do now, I would have cried it out on the bathroom floor then walked upstairs, shared my concerns with my family and planned to talk with a mental health professional as soon as possible.

Instead, you'll hatch a plan. You'll ignore the intuitive crescendo in your head. You'll think, *the coast highway isn't far away.* You'll grab your running shoes, throw on a jacket and head for the back door. You'll think, *I could run across the rain-soaked pavement, step into the path of a logging truck and end it all.*

You'll get as far as slipping on your shoes and tying the laces. Your mom will call downstairs to check on you. The sound of her voice will shatter your resolve. You'll know that you can't go through with the plan. You can't do that to her. It'll be the only thought that cuts through your profound shame and despair. You can't hurt *her.*

A few days later you'll start the drive back to California. The sharp urge to end your life will have ebbed slightly but it'll hang on you like a shadow, constantly dogging your thoughts. The promise of relief from the self-shaming, the self-bullying will seem so clear and seductive.

Sitting in the passenger seat, watching the trees flash by, the bile will rise up in your throat and you feel a powerful urge to open the door to throw yourself out of the moving car. You'll started sobbing, much to the chagrin of your partner.

Choking and sputtering, you'll tell him the thoughts coursing through your head. Once you start, you won't be able to stop. It'll be a torrent of despair, of self-hatred. He'll listen. He'll hold your hand. You'll agree that it is time to speak with a professional.

Fair to say, you'll be scared. Scared of *not* losing these thoughts of self-harm and despair. And, scared of *losing* them. After all, at least when you're in pain, you know you're alive, right? You'll be scared of surviving. And, scared about *not* surviving. Scared about what you'll find out about yourself. It'll be a long drive home – full of love and even some laughs – and by the time you pull into the driveway, you'll start to believe that there could be a way to rise from the deep.

Two months after that car ride, you'll find yourself sitting on a couch in the front room, staring out the window. You'll have started therapy with a wonderful and compassionate therapist. You'll have a safe space to share your feelings and sort through the list of damaging self-narratives.

Rather than the loud, bullying voices that'd increasingly ruled your life for the past several years, you'll start to hear a calm, loving voice. Your ever-patient *intuition*. Your True Self. That gentle voice will guide you towards the surface and out of the darkness.

You'll stumble across a listing for a coaching school while looking for new jobs – something you'll do compulsively every time your world is shaken up.

Coaching. It'll sound pretty woo-woo. They'll talk about energy and changing mindsets; it'll sound like psychobabble and, honestly, kinda like a scam. You'll be intrigued but, as a scientist, this program will seem like selling snake oil. *At best.*

That inner voice will persist. You'll remember the danger of ignoring that intuition (remember when you ignored your own pleas to get help, to get out of destructive patterns, to listen), so you'll fill out an inquiry form. An hour later you'll have an appointment with an admissions rep. A day later, you'll be enrolled in the coaching certification program.

It'll all seem to move so quickly. Like, suspiciously quickly. Trust it. Trust the ease. This is the decision that will change your life.

Trust your gut when it tells you something is wrong.

Trust your intuition when it says something, or someone isn't good for you.

Life Lesson Challenges

- When in your life have you ignored your intuition? When have you not acted on *gut feelings* or *hunches*, in the past?
- Looking back, what would you do or think differently?
- Looking forward, what can your intuition tell you? What lessons can you identify from the patterns in your life, around intuition?

LIFE LESSON 2

I Wish I Knew That Breaking Down Often Means Breaking Through

originally titled this chapter *Breaking Down Means Breaking Through*. I re-titled it after realizing that some people could interpret this to mean that *breakdowns* are necessary to transforming your mindset. I'm defining breakdown as a collapse of my normal emotional functioning and a sense of profound inertia. I personally believe that charting a new course of your life, owning your story, and making conscious choices requires new neurological patterns, i.e., breaking habits, disproving limiting beliefs, etc. Some people may experience emotional and psychological reshuffling during that patterning; they may indeed suffer a *breakdown*. During these times, I usually feel very sad, lost, uncertain, afraid, and alone. These breakdowns can last for a few hours or a few weeks. I don't think that is the only road to transformation, but it is a road some must travel. If you are experiencing chronic, repeated, unresolvable emotional and psychological distress, I urge you to reach out to qualified mental health practitioners and coaches to help you through that dark night of the soul. I've been there, and having trusted guides made a huge difference to me during my most difficult moments. You aren't alone and don't need to walk that path by yourself.

🍍 🍍 🍍 🍍 🍍 🍍

Dear Lisa,

You'll make it through those dark times. You'll survive that breakdown and enroll in the coaching program.

Ten days after your call with that admissions rep, you'll be sitting in a rental car in the snow-crusted parking lot outside a Minneapolis hotel, trying to figure out how the hell you'd gotten there. You'll be reeling from your breakdown a few weeks earlier in Oregon; your emotions and psyche rubbed raw.

When you sign up for the program they'll tell you that you've missed the San Francisco training, but they'll find you a place in the Minneapolis group. Which makes perfect sense, since your sister and her family live in the Twin Cities now. And, you'll find a cheap non-stop flight. You'll have a coupon for a week's free rental car. And you'll get upgraded to first class upon arrival at the airport.

Just like the scheduling of that initial admissions call, everything will proceed seamlessly, effortlessly. Even pleasantly. It'll be hard to trust that ease.

Sitting in that rental car, you'll be panicking. The car engine will be running. You'll be shaking (and not just because it is freezing outside) and sweating.

This is a tipping point.

You can either turn off the car, walk inside, and start this training; or, you can put the car in gear, drive back to your sister's house and explain why you aren't going through with it.

This will be your first battle of Thermopylae (you know, when 300 Spartans fought, vastly-outnumbered by a Persian army; the quintessential tale of valor in the face of certain defeat). Sitting in that lukewarm rental car on a cold, crisp Minnesota morning, it will feel like you are facing a million, razor sharp spears. You could march against a foe with seemingly unbeatable force (your shame tapes around failure, inadequacy, not-enough-ness), face certain defeat (death of your ego), with honor; or turn tail and live as an outcast, disowned and rejected (let the shame win).

After a few minutes of deep breathing, you'll turn off the car engine, crunch across the snow, and walk into that hotel. Your heart will be pounding, your knees weak, like you were indeed walking towards Xerxes' vast army.

That first day of coach training won't convert you. You'll be skeptical, cynical, and scared. You won't have yet tasted the full power of expanding your consciousness, increasing your self-awareness, or controlling your self-dialogue. It will be excruciatingly difficult to be vulnerable in front of these strangers. You will put on your *funny-confidant* armor, cracking jokes, making a show of playing along, trying to convince everyone you knew your own mind.

It will all be a front. You'll be scared shitless and convinced that you have sunk your hard-earned money into some crackpot get-rich-quick scheme, or worse, some snake-oil selling, crystal-dancing, woo-woo cult. You aren't quite ready for this breakthrough. *Yet.*

You'll be unwilling to believe that what you're being taught will make a difference. You'll ask yourself, *how could this coaching shit help anyone?* You'll feel like you've been scammed. You'll feel embarrassed that you bought into all this marketing bullshit. Your shame tapes will start up again. Driving back to your sister's house after that first day, you'll be convinced you aren't going back for Day Two or Day Three.

You'll wake up the next morning resigned. You won't be able to bear losing face by not heading back to the hotel and you're pretty sure they won't refund your money if you don't at least go through the motions. So, you sit through Day Two. Head nodding, taking notes, making chit-chat, you'll try to play along with the practice coaching drills, all the while feeling the pit in your stomach sink lower and lower. That night, you'll cry yourself to sleep, overwhelmed with grief, uncertainty, and something approaching despair. This is a necessary step of each breakdown: letting yourself feel what you need to feel. Caging and restraining the feelings only increases their power. Unleash them. Let yourself be sad. Cry, yell, whatever you need to do, in order to set those feelings free. Trust that this is a necessary part of the breakdown process.

The morning of Day Three will dawn cold but bright; the last training day of this first module. Feeling hungover from last night's emotional storm, you'll walk into that meeting room fully expecting to put your armor back on, make jokes, share enough of yourself so folks think you are along for the ride, but not so much that they'll have weapons to use against you. You still see everything as win or lose. Viking or victim.

Something very miraculous will happen that morning. You won't see strangers anymore. You won't automatically snap on that victim-Viking lens. You won't see yourself as separate, the *other*, isolated, or alone. That morning, in a nondescript Minneapolis hotel room, you'll realize that you have found your tribe. Something will begin to shift deep in your psyche, and you'll see your fellow trainees for who they really are: smart, successful, caring people. Not broken. Not defeated. Not gullible. They are people seeking to find their way out of their own abyss while also seeking to help others rise. Trust these people. They will help you in so many ways. They are your tribe.

When the day's training starts, you won't *just* play along. You'll actually be enjoying yourself, you will see the potential of what you're learning and understand the gift you've been given.

This will be the first real chink in your armor. This is just the first of many revelations that you'll experience as a result of starting your journey of self-acceptance, self-awareness, and self-actualization. You'll let yourself believe that maybe, just maybe, all this marketing b.s. wasn't b.s. after all. You'll start to believe that maybe you aren't irredeemable.

You'll start to believe in *you*. This will feel odd and a little uncomfortable. Hang in there, it'll get easier.

You'll go back to Minneapolis for the second and third modules that year. Each time you walk into that hotel meeting room, it will be like walking into Shangri-La. Your tribe will be back together; sharing war stories, hugging, crying (there'll be lots of crying), and laughing (there'll be lots of laughing).

Now, lest you leave this chapter thinking this part of your journey will be all unicorns and rainbows, I want to be clear: this training will require you to do deep, difficult, emotional and spiritual work.

All these breakthroughs will force you to confront your shame tapes, head on. You'll sit in the middle of the room and share your deepest darkest fears. Out loud. On more than one occasion. You'll come to terms with the fact that *you* are the only one holding you back. You'll realize that you were the invisible hand forcing you into the abyss.

It wasn't you against the world. *It was you against yourself*. This is the ultimate breakthrough.

Every day you'll feel more and more connected to that Universal fabric you used to scoff at (admittedly, from a place of deep scarcity and fear).

And, since that sunny, cold, Sunday morning, you'll never feel alone again. You'll never feel like you're floating in darkness, unable to see the light. Because of this work and this tribe, you'll know that you can and do create your own light.

And, you'll see there's so much light, so much energy and joy to go around. You'll be so glad you finally listened to that calm, patient voice. You'll be so thankful the Universe led you to this path, this life, this future.

This is your calling. This is what you're meant to do.

You'll be so grateful that you will have the incredible privilege of helping others find and shine their light too; to help them the swim up from the deep.

Life Lesson Challenges
- Have you experienced breakthroughs in your life? How and when did they take place?
- What did those breakthroughs feel like? What is the same every time? What cues does your mind, body, and intuition send you during these times?
- What did you learn as a result of the breakthrough(s)? How are you implementing these learnings into your life?
- What does support look like for you, during the breakdowns? How would it feel to share that information with loved ones and your tribe?
- How can you cultivate that *breakthrough* feeling every day?

LIFE LESSON 3

I Wish I Knew That Journaling Opens a Door to the Universe

Journaling is a constant surprise to me. It seems like such a simple recipe, right? Pen. Paper. A few minutes of undisturbed time. And yet, within its simplicity is a spiritual superhighway to my Higher Self and Universal guidance. A humble pen and a scrap of paper connecting to the Universal fabric? Seems wacky and I don't blame you for being skeptical. In my experience, when I'm feeling mentally stuck or emotionally entrenched, taking a few minutes to scribble what's racing through my head opens that door to my Higher Self. It gets me unstuck and digs me out of those analysis-paralysis situations. I invite you to explore journaling as part of your daily practices (if you don't already) and see what opening that Universal portal brings to your life.

Hint, hint: there may be some awesome journaling questions at the end of each chapter and a free downloadable workbook to guide you in working through the lessons in this book (go to siwiky-book.com for all the good stuff!)

* * * * * *

Dear Lisa,

I know you're already doing this (as in, I know you talk to yourself) but I'm here to up the ante. I'm inviting you to start putting those thoughts and inner monologues down on paper. Go beyond verbally talking to yourself while driving/running/biking/showering/walking the dog and start putting that sh*t out into the Universe. Start journaling!

It'll take you a long time to figure out what all the fuss is about journaling. You'll think, *you are sitting and writing things in a journal? For what? To what end*? The thought of sitting still at a desk, pen scratching across the paper for the better part of an hour will send cold chills of terror down your spine. It'll seem so pointless. I get that! Let me tell you a story.

A few months after finishing your coach training, you'll find yourself at a retreat sitting on a chair in a spacious room next to a crackling fire, surrounded by fellow seekers. Your facilitator will give the group a few prompts to address during free journaling time.

You'll write them down and then just stare at the blank paper. Holding the journal, opened to a blank page, gripping a pen and you'll freeze. *What the hell am I supposed to write*, you'll wonder silently. All around you people will be scribbling furiously and purposefully.

Crap. You'll start to panic a bit.

Your pen will hover but not have the courage to actually hit the page. You'll feel time ticking by. The fire will snap and one of the logs will fall deeper into the glowing embers. You'll almost feel the words being written around you like hands pressing on your arms and shoulders.

Nothing will come to you. Not. One. Single. Thing.

You'll try to come up with filler bullshit just to mark up the page. Frustration and envy will tear through you.

You'll start to berate yourself and ask, *"Who are these people? How do they know what to write? What's wrong with you that you can't seem to do this?"* Your inner teacher's pet will throw a full-on temper tantrum. There's no way you're getting an A on this assignment.

Going to this retreat will seem like an indulgence several months ago when you signed up on a whim. It'll be your first retreat and you'll have no idea what to expect. It will be one of your first attempts to listen to your intuition, without judgement; the intuitive decision to go will make no sense. You'll anticipate a lot of group chanting, probably some mental exercises, possible yoga and definitely meditation. You aren't against any of those things per se, but paying your good money for that—versus just re-creating it for free at your house –it'll seem a little far-fetched and fiscally irresponsible (more on the dangers of scarcity mindset later!).

Fast forward to finding yourself sitting on that chair, holding the blank journal and an equally blank mind; it'll feel like your return on this investment might be in single digits. At best.

You'll enjoy the conversation and make new connections with fascinating people. But that blank journal will haunt you. You'll go to bed that night feeling a little forlorn and unsettled.

The next morning, inspired to move, you'll start walking and find that your feet just sorta intuitively steer you down to the beach. Standing just off the boardwalk, toes buried in the cold, deep sand, you'll breath in the salty air.

It'll be exactly what you need. *Score two for your intuition.* You'll feel something reset in those few breaths, something fundamental. Like that scene in movies where the actor/actress closes their eyes, breathes deeply, and snaps open their eyes, a different person, different colored-eyes, new powers, whatever the storyline needs. You'll feel re-booted.

You'll sit down a few hours later, surrounded once again by your fellow seekers, next to the same crackling fire, underneath the cozy wooden, beamed ceiling. That re-booted feeling will only deepen.

To say everything will seem clearer and sharper will sound like a cliché; but, truly, that's what it'll seem like. It'll feel like when you wore corrective lens for the first time: whole worlds opened up, in three-dimensions, with depth and clarity.

When the time comes to write in the journals, you'll get up from your chair and walk to the corner of the room, lowering yourself onto a floor cushion. Even before you open the journal to a fresh page, you'll feel words and phrases starting to bubble up in your mind. Writing will seem elemental, inseparable from your soul. It is a conversation with your Higher Self. The pen scratches furiously across the paper; you'll quite literally feel the words flowing from your fingers. They won't be your words. It'll feel more like you are a conduit. The words appear on the page without making a pitstop in your frontal cortex.

So, will it really be that easy? Taking a few deep breaths of morning ocean air and the world of journaling opens up to you? Yes and no.

Yes, because in that peri-dawn moment, standing on cold sand, watching the waves glitter as they broke against the shore, you'll set the intention – although you won't be aware of it at the time – to stop second-guessing everything you do or think.

You'll give yourself permission to fully experience this retreat.

You'll resolve to enter the remaining sessions with an open mind, trying to take in that which would uncover your true self and reject the thoughts, feelings, and actions that armor you up. That's certainly a point in the win column.

And no, because, although you'll find things to write that morning (and for the rest of the weekend), you'll often find yourself wanting external validation for those thoughts. You'll want to post them publicly for everyone to critique and condone. It'll feel like a challenge levied by the Universe: learn how to do this (journaling), and keep it to yourself, and see what happens. This challenge will force you to confront a truth: at this point in your life, external validation carries more weight than internal belief. Not wanting this to be true, you'll dive headlong into exploring how to care more about what you think, than what others think.

Weeks later – challenge accepted – you'll fear you've tipped the scales into journaling obsession. Every morning, you'll sit down with your coffee and scratch out page after page after page. You'll learn to set a timer so that you'll have a stopping point; without that alarm, you'll probably write all day.

Here's why this is so important: the act of journaling will change you, change the way you walk through the world, change the way you see yourself and your calling. You'll sometimes catch yourself during the day thinking, "I'm gonna journal on that!" or, "Maybe journaling will help me find the answers."

Journaling is one way you'll connect with the Universe each day, tapping into that heady combination of intuition, intellect, and mastery.

It's a conversation with yourself, with your Higher Self, the one who *Knows* everything that will happen, the one with the inside track and short-cuts to your desired future. And like any conversation, it's a back-n-forth affair: question and answer, inquiry and response.

And like any great conversation, you'll feel incredibly enriched when the talking is over.

Life Lesson Challenges

Here are some prompts to get you started in the practice of journaling. Why not try to answer these questions every day, first thing in the morning, for a week and see what happens? Open up a fresh page in your journal, pick a prompt, and free write for 20 mins (I set a timer on my phone!).

- "I'm pretending not to know that _____"
- "_____ in my life is waiting to be acknowledged and loved."
- "I want to feel _____ when I do _____ today/this week"
- What practice(s) do you have to connect with your inner guidance? If none, why not?
- What practice would you like to try? Journaling? Audio notes? What's stopping you?
- How does your journaling practice influence your life?
- How can you bring your journaling practice to the next level?

LIFE LESSON 4

I Wish I Knew That Judgement Was Really All About My Sh*t, Not Theirs

et's be clear about one thing: judgement is a human condition and is, arguably, necessary for survival. I'd like to introduce a term I wish I'd known earlier in my life: discernment. Judgment and discernment are cousins. They both describe the process of identifying and perceiving difference. However, crucially, discernment is perception of difference *without judgement*. Judgement is the process of sorting things, people, events, into buckets: good or bad, right or wrong. Again, judgement can be really helpful in certain moments. Staying in judgement – or living a lifestyle powered by judgement, especially when you're not aware of it – can really degrade one's ability to stay present, be happy, and experience gratitude. Wait, does that sound like a judgement? Nope, it's discernment. I'm not telling you that you're a bad person to live your life judging yourself and others. I'm saying it's a lifestyle that will likely lead to detachment, dissatisfaction, and unhappiness. Only you can decide if that supports your life goals or not.

🍍 🍍 🍍 🍍 🍍 🍍

Dear Lisa,

Let me you tell you a story.

A few years from now, you'll find yourself sitting across from a woman at a meeting. She's about your age and worked for the firm you're visiting. You'll have the impression that she was from a wealthy upbringing. She'll exude confidence and poise. You find yourself thinking, "She's never known a hard day in her life." It'll make you feel powerful to judge her, to set your rocky life story in distinct relief to hers. You'll feel like a survivor. You tell yourself that's she's just some rich kid who fell ass-backwards into money and privilege.

Two hours later, the meeting will end, and as you reached for your notebook, your pen will fall from your grasp, and roll under the table. Kneeling down to retrieve it, you'll look up and your stomach will jolt with shock. Peeking under the hem of her work pants is an artificial foot.

Instead of the smooth creamy skin you'll expected to see, her right foot was beige, plasticky and stiff. You'll feel sick.

She'll meet your self-conscious gaze with a knowing look. But you won't be able to hold her gaze and the lump in your throat with harden.

You try to stop yourself from watching her walk out of the building, without a noticeable limp, a few yards in front of you.

Later that night, you finally work up the courage to apologize to her for your behavior. She'll tell you the whole story.

She was ten years old. It was late summer. Her family lived in a working-class neighborhood. Italian family. Close. Gregarious. It was one of those blocks were the kids would play soccer in the streets until sunset, creating makeshift goals of buckets and bookbags. A bunch of her friends were standing on the corner watching their cousins play keep-away with a baseball. She saw a flash of light over her right shoulder and then felt a rush of air.

A speeding car jumped the curb and plowed into her and her friends. One second, it was a sunlit, perfect evening. The next second, she was floating in a haze of pain, the smell of hot metal and gasoline enveloping her. She said she didn't remember much about those moments. She knew she was lying on her back because she could feel the grit and gravel under her bare shoulders – she'd been wearing a favorite sundress that day.

Time flashed by in snatches; snapshots of color, sound, and sensation.

She was in the hospital for three months. They had to remove most of her right leg. She had third degree burns on her shoulder and chest where the car's engine seared her skin. She never wore bathing suits. She never went to the beach. She tried for a while, but the stares and whispers were too much for her. Three of her friends were killed, several more severely injured. The driver of the car was a woman who lived three streets away; she'd had a fight with her husband and driven away from their house in a drunken rage. The car was traveling 80 mph when it hit the curb.

So, you'll listen to her tell this story in a matter-of-fact way, gripping your glass convulsively, as tears pour down your face.

This creature sitting in front of you, dressed in a smart business suit, with gorgeous long hair and a perfect smile was the epitome of bravery and survival.

Not just for her looks. For what you believed to be her backstory; what you'd assumed had been her *perfect* childhood. Before hearing the truth, you reveled in the judgement that she had never known real fear, or suffering, or courage.

You'll talk with her for a long time that night.

You'll apologize. You tell her you've been judging her the whole day. You tell her that you were making yourself feel better, stronger, more capable, more heroic by assuming she'd had it easy. You'll brace yourself for her – very understandable – burst of anger.

She laughs. She laughs so loud and for so long that the rest of the group pause and turn to stare at you both. Ignoring them completely, she wipes the tears off her face and nods. She got it. She knew. You haven't been fooling anyone. She knew, because it happened to her. Every. Damn. Day.

She knew that people took one look at her flawless skin and long, wavy hair and wrote her off. She knew that they had no idea what it had taken that ten-year-old to come back from a tragedy that would've levelled anyone.

She knew that people wouldn't understand her PTSD flashbacks on the subway, when the smell of hot brakes and mechanical fluids rushed her back to the summer evening, broken and hurt in so many ways, pinned to the concrete by someone else's rage. She knew that people wouldn't believe her until she proved it by lifting up her pant leg. She knew that they'd lob pity at her instead of empathy because they weren't willing to climb into that darkness with her. They weren't willing to climb into that hospital bed, into the rehab unit, into the prosthetics labs. Into those horrible, painful moments in the high school gym where she had to watch her friends live out her dream of playing basketball.

You're one of those people who have to learn lessons the hard way. And you'll learn your lesson on judging people that day. The hard way.

Because you can never really know someone's story until they share it. Anything you tell yourself about that person or their journey is more about *you* than it is about them.

It's like taking all your emotional baggage, throwing it over to them, and telling them to carry it for you. Judging people from what we can see is like telling yourself that only the top two inches of sea water are the entire ocean. It's convenient, because then we don't have to bother diving into the waters to figure out what else is down there.

But, it's the easy way out. It's the chicken sh*t way out. And even as powerful as this lesson was for you, you'll still find yourself staying too long in judgement, especially self-judgment, over the years.

We are all deeper and more complex than those top inches of sea water. We all have dark canyons, fear lurking in the shadows. No one rides for free.

Judging other people (or yourself!) and holding those thoughts in your body slowly erodes your soul. It's caustic. It holds you back from fully experiencing life. Living your life free (or 99% free, no one's perfect!) of judgement, you'll find it easier to connect with people, to live your life with grace, and to fully experience abundance. Who wouldn't want that?

Life Lesson Challenges
- When do you find yourself judging people? Why? What is this costing you?
- When do spend time judging yourself? Why? What is this costing you?

- What would change in your life, if you stopped judging? How would that feel?
- What would non-judgement sound and look like?
- What benefits do you see from reducing self-judgement in your life?

LIFE LESSON 5

I Wish I Knew to Appreciate Struggle

Not Resist It

This is another paradox: learning to love and appreciate the hard times. The journey to higher consciousness and self-awareness seems full of paradoxes. I'm certainly not the first (or last) person to describe this phenomenon. After all, the cliché *it's always darkest before the dawn* exists for a reason (Life Lesson #31 dives into this concept more deeply). During one challenging moment I actually wrote a love letter to struggle. Check it out at the back of the book. This lesson also dovetails with Life Lesson #2 on breaking down to breakthrough. It's all about not resisting the *breaking down* times, believing that we will survive it, and trusting that the breaking through will happen. When we can appreciate the struggles we're experiencing, we invite the dawn and the insights that are on their way to us.

Hence, my argument for appreciating what's showing up in our lives, using them as spiritual breadcrumbs to make our way through to the other side.

* * * * * *

Dear Lisa,

It may sound strange that I'm inviting you to *love* struggle. *Isn't struggle the thing you've been trying to avoid your whole life?* You could be forgiven for feeling skeptical.

I hear you. But, given all the things I've advised you on before, it's not really that surprising, is it? And, I'm talking here about the *existential* struggle, emotional and spiritual skirmish, not actual fights. That's a whole, different book.

Here's my challenge to you—what if that *struggle* is really your intuition and wisdom trying to get your attention? What if they've tried every other way to get the message across and it isn't working?

There's a saying floating around that says pain is inevitable, but suffering is optional. Meaning, that life will throw some curve balls your way; some of those curve balls will be full of pain. Losing a loved one. Cancer. Ending relationships. All of these events cause pain. If you resist that pain, rather than letting yourself accept and acknowledge it, you will suffer. This isn't about faking positivity.

I'm inviting you to recognize that things are difficult and sit with it. Acknowledge that's difficult and ask yourself why; get curious about the underlying causes for your struggle.

Here's an example of how this will show up in your life.

You will go through a divorce. Understandably, this will be

a time of deep emotional pain and turmoil. At the time, you'll seek to dispel that intense discomfort by blaming others (and yourself) and transferring the pain. This pain is inevitable, but you don't have the awareness yet to realize that no amount of ignoring it, business, deflection or false positivity can extinguish it.

Desperate to escape what seems like punishing proximity and shame, you take a job that requires you to move to Minneapolis. In that first year of separation – after seven years of marriage - there will be moments of intense self-doubt and self-blame. Rumination will occupy a lot of your time. You resist the urge to cry or seem unhappy at all, even though you'll fool no one with this facade.

You'll feel the urge to lean into your grief but worry about getting so deep into that emotional well that you can't get out. You will berate yourself for wanting to wallow (which in your mind is a source of shame) for wanting to grieve. Instead, you will throw yourself into the new job and work constantly.

Without an outlet, the grief will build up in your body and psyche, choking you. *Nope everything is great*, you'll tell people, *the divorce is the best thing that ever happened to me*.

All that suppressed grief and self-blame will boil over, as it always does. You'll just have arrived back at your apartment in Minneapolis after a punishing four days of travel. Your throat will feel constricted, like someone is truly choking you, and you'll feel the walls around your grief begin to crumble. It's a bitterly cold day in January. The wind will be howling outside, snow swirling furiously around, tapping against the glass not unlike the tapping inside your head: your intuition is trying to get your attention.

The deluge will happen without warning. The tears will fall, sobs erupting, your throat constricting even more, emotions coursing over you like powerful waves. You'll fall to the cold concrete floor, distraught and incapable of mounting any resistance. Your dog, Solo, will lay by you. The two of you will sit there for nearly an hour, sobs and keening consuming your body, months' worth of bottled grief finally unleashed.

Eventually, you'll open your eyes. The snowfall has increased and outside your window is a monochromatic wonderland. Without really thinking, you'll change into warm, cozy clothes, grab a fluffy quilt and climb into the chair by your window. Solo will climb up next to you. And, together, silently, you'll watch the snow fall and the sky darken. As sad as you are, as heavy as the unleashed grief feels, you'll start to notice something else emerging: a sense of clarity, opportunity, of being cleansed. You'll know that you'll survive this, that the notion of giving into your feelings is worse than the actual experience.

These moments are like GPS for our souls, for our destiny. And, importantly, they are pressure release valves for our emotions. Accepting how you feel and giving into the desire to experience those emotions actually gets you from point A (struggle) to point B (not struggling) faster than resistance. Leaning into that *struggle* will help guide you towards your next step, the next decisions. It'll reveal the clarity buried deep down in a blanket of emotional free-for-all. You just have to ride out the storm.

Bottom line: accepting struggle as a part of life and allowing yourself to experience the emotions that ride shotgun with struggle, is the fastest, most direct route to the life you want.

Have courage, and lean in.

Life Lesson Challenges
- What's your view of the struggles that come into your life?
- If you are struggling with struggle, how might that resistance be holding you back?
- How would your life change if you explored the discomfort rather than sought to quell it immediately?
- What could these struggles be trying to tell you?

LIFE LESSON 6

I Wish I Knew How to Live
My Future in the Present

I wrote this chapter before completely devouring Dr. Joe Dispenza's book *Becoming Supernatural* (Hay House Inc, ISBN 9781401953119). Dr. Dispenza and others describe brilliantly the process of connecting with future realities that already exist for us. I'm not going to do that here. My intention with this lesson is to help my younger self (and you, readers!) appreciate that you can act, feel, and live as though that reality has already arrived. I think you'll see what I mean as you read on.

Dear Lisa,

The big, beautiful journey you're on is worth the trip. No question.

However, that doesn't mean you have to take backroads the whole way if you don't want to. Why not mentally fast forward to point B now?

More specifically, I'm inviting you to look down the road, bottle all the experiences and feelings you'll have at that future point and drink it now.

Let me operationalize this for you.

For example, in a few years, you will discover triathlon and fall in love with the sport. Every race you finish you'll feel a surge of pride, confidence, accomplishment, and invincibility. What if you decided to feel all those things today?

If you knew success, love, and joy were right around the corner for you, what would you do differently? Right now.

No race, no finish line. No running, biking, swimming required.

Just decide to feel proud, confident, accomplished. Invincible. All the time.

You have the power to do that. You have 100% control of your emotions.

Why not feel today the way you want to feel in the future? It's the ultimate short-cut.

I invite you to try the following:
- Cast your mind five years into the future, where and when you're living your dream life.
  - What are you doing?
  - How are you feeling?
  - Where do you live?
  - What car are you driving?
  - Be as specific as possible, seriously, and have fun!
- Dream big – the point is, your future is unlimited (as

are you), so this is not the time to be putting so-called 'reality blinkers' on your vision.

- Now have a conversation with that Future version of yourself.
  - What would Future You tell the Present You to do or say?
  - What would Future You tell the Present You not to worry about?
  - How would Future You coach you to take action in your life?
- What would you worry less about, knowing what's in store for you?
- Try this every day for two weeks and notice how much that shift in mindset, that transportation of your consciousness into a joyous, abundant future state impacts how you show up today.

Life Lesson Challenges

- How easy is it for you to envision your ideal future? What does it look like? How many specific details can you imagine? (Hint: the more specific, the better!)
- What would be different if you truly believed that ideal future is a certainty? How would you act? What would you feel?
- What is your current skepticism (around not getting the life you want) costing you? Where is it holding you back?
- Ask yourself, "What would my Future Self want me to stop, start, or continue?"

LIFE LESSON 7

I Wish I Knew How to Accept My Flawsomeness and Be Seen

'm a big fan of words. I have my favorites, sure, like anyone. Kerplunk. Kerflooey. Basically, anything that begins with *ker*. Seriously though, this lesson is about more than just a great word—flawsome. It's really about self-acceptance, especially in the face of external criticism. I'll revisit this concept throughout the book, starting with this idea of *being seen*. It really boils down to a (sadly) over-used word: authenticity. Showing up authentically, who you are, where you are, when you are. There's so much power in that and, yes, it requires vulnerability and courage.

🍍 🍍 🍍 🍍 🍍 🍍

Dear Lisa,

Be seen.

Lesson over, right? If only it was that easy. Let me explain.

Being seen is just what it sounds like: showing the world your *authentic* self. Your whole self.

(Note—I'm not advocating over-sharing or opening the curtains to your entire life. That's not what authenticity really is.)

I know how hard it is for you to have your picture taken. You scurry away from family photos or, really, anyone holding a camera.

You hate every photo of you.

You'll burn piles of photographs of you because you can only see your flaws, your faults, your perceived imperfections.

You'll destroy huge swaths of your history. You'll regret this action.

You'll sit quietly during meetings, not willing to raise your hand, not willing to speak up or be seen. It's so much easier being invisible, right?

I know that belief is driven by a powerful shame tape around not feeling beautiful, not feeling *worthy* of being seen.

I'm inviting you to start shifting that mindset now.

Flawsome is all about loving yourself for your imperfections rather than in spite of them. It's reveling in the unique, wonderous, one-in-seven-billion miracle that is each human existence. Flawsome and authenticity go hand-in-hand. When you decide to show up authentically, you'll start to accept who you are: perfectly flawed. Flawsome.

This is an invitation to cultivate an impregnable sense of self-acceptance, worthiness and belonging by speaking lovingly to yourself. Are those flaws you see *really* flaws? Are they actually the things that make you unique and wonderful? How can you celebrate them? What would you say to a friend who talked to herself in the same words you use (ugly, weird, freak)? What would you tell her mattered most about your friendship (spoiler alert—it's not her hair or the way her eyebrows look)?

Oh, and, we're all flawed. It's part of the deal. People who think they don't have flaws are lying to themselves and you.

When you start stepping into this acceptance, you'll stop fearing how others see you. You'll feel a sense of profound freedom in the way you move, speak, dress, and express yourself.

Self-acceptance is a necessary prerequisite to up-leveling your life and truly pursuing those dreams.

Life Lesson Challenges
- How would it feel to accept your *flawsomeness* wholeheartedly?
- Which public figures do you admire? Why? What lessons can you take from their willingness to be been?
- What would change in your life? What would be different for you?
- If you've already mastered this lesson, what helped you get there? How can you support folks in your life that may be struggling?

LIFE LESSON 8

I Wish I Knew I was Braver
than I Realized

B ravery. A word that's rife with connotations, probably conjuring images of heroes and heroines leaping off tall buildings, swashbuckling, and slacklining above a 3,000-foot drop. You get the point. What we don't talk about often is that bravery and its emotional counterpart, courage, is needed to face our everyday lives. We need bravery to show up every day in our lives: to be an employee, a dedicated parent and partner, to love someone, to achieve goals. Without courage, we would let fear dictate our actions and inaction. I didn't realize this for a long time. I thought bravery had to be 1) celebrated externally and 2) all about extreme actions. Looking back on my life, I realize (and celebrate) that I am indeed brave and live my life courageously. Not by swashbuckling but by showing up, by rising to the challenge, by listening to my intuition, and for not compromising on my dreams. I have a feeling if you look back at *your* life with this filter, you'll realize that you, too, are much braver than you realize.

♣ ♣ ♣ ♣ ♣ ♣

Dear Lisa,

You always thought of yourself as a brave person because you did (and will do) things others are afraid to try. Like move to new cities or places every few years. Like compete in IRONMAN races.

Now, I'm not saying those things didn't take courage, but standing up for yourself during a performance review with your boss will also require bravery. Your knees will shake, you will sweat through your shirt, your voice will tremble and falter. But you will show up and ask for what you deserve. You won't think of it as bravery, but that's what it is.

You will feel that same tremble of fear when you ask someone out on a date for the first time after your divorce. And when he turns you down, it will take bravery to walk right back into that coffee shop the next day, order your usual latte, and act as though nothing is wrong, even though your heart is thumping in your chest and your stomach is brimming with anxiety.

You won't be on the traditional front lines of warfare or battle. For those of us who have chosen non-soldier paths, the million acts of courage we perform each day may not stand out in the crowd. But courage is a part of your daily life. Like everyone around you. It takes courage to wake up, chase your dreams, and face the possibility of failure.

But you'll do that over and over again in your life.

You'll start companies that don't make a profit. Like the bakery business. The idea of starting and operating a home-based bakery business in a 700-square-foot house with a 1950's kitchen, no dishwasher, and a foot of counter space will seem insurmountable. You will tackle all the paperwork. You will find a way to rearrange the furniture. You will encounter problems, feel the fear of uncertainty, and seek solutions. You will repeat this cycle over and over again, until you find yourself proudly standing behind a table laden with homemade pies, cookies, and breads, under a tent at the local market. You will be afraid of people hating your baked goods, but you will do it anyway. You'll charge, undaunted, into this unknown. And when, a few years down the road, it's clear that the bakery business isn't sustainable as a one woman show, you will have the courage to change your mind, close the bakery, and be open to the next step on your journey.

I'm here to tell you, *definitively* — you are brave.

You are courageous.

You are the bravest person I know.

Keep it up. The life you want to live takes courage.

Life Lesson Challenges
- What does bravery mean to you?
- When do you feel most courageous?
- How do you acknowledge and celebrate your bravery?
- What would it feel like to own your courage and step into all your life experiences with that deep awareness of bravery?

LIFE LESSON 9

I Wish I Knew What It Felt like When the Universe was Trying to Get My Attention

I'm using the word *Universe* where others may prefer Source, God, Divinity. Essentially, this is a concept of something higher, bigger than our current, present reality. An omnipotent force. There are lots of lessons to learn about interacting and embracing an expansive view of the humane experience. For me, as a lifelong skeptic, it took a while to digest and appreciate the concept of a Universe, beyond the astronomical or physical reality. I now consider myself a very spiritual person; it was, and continues to be, a journey of many steps. As I work to accept and cultivate my spirituality even more deeply, I'm learning to hear the Universal call more clearly. In some things I'm a slow learner. But, I'm learning.

Dear Lisa,

I'd love to tell you that, because of your training and life experience, you'll recognize these Universal calls to action, walk through a golden beam of light and emerge on the other side, enlightened.

Not so much.

Instead, this is what it feels like when the Universe is trying to get your attention:

- You fall – literally and figuratively.
- You constantly feel like you're playing a game of metaphysical hide-and-seek.
- You feel constantly unsettled.
- You'll keep trying new things, anything, to find your place in the world.
- You'll feel completely vulnerable, naked in the maelstrom of fate, destined to perish by a thousand cuts, a thousand mistakes.
- Your intuition keeps nudging you about things (remember that lesson about ignoring intuition?).

So, what does it mean to recognize Universal calls to action? Why does this help you?

It helps you fast forward to the next step in your journey and it may prevent you from going down some existential rabbit holes. It's easier to recognize Universal turn signals retrospectively. I'm inviting you to recognize them in the moment.

These Universal bulletins are that you are either, 1) onto something big that's gonna crack open your reality or, 2) you are way out of alignment with your soul GPS and need to re-route.

I Wish I Knew What It Felt like When the Universe was Trying to Get My Attention

Suffice to say, when you are onto something big – like following your intuition and up-leveling your existence – the Universe will leave some tasty breadcrumbs on your path. More on that later.

Let's tackle the out-of-alignment scenario.

One day, a few years from now, you will fall. Literally. You will jump into the shower, rushing to clean up because you are late for a client meeting, and you will fall, losing consciousness for a few seconds. Coming to, ass over elbows in the bathtub, you will be pretty stunned. You'll have concussion, a bruised elbow and a contused hip. It happens, right?

Four days later, you will be walking around the yard, enjoying the fresh air while obsessing about the marketing report you need to send a client. You'll be so deep in analysis-paralysis that you won't recognize – until it's too late – that your dog is running full speed at you, in pursuit of the squirrel sitting a few feet behind you. So, you'll fall again. You'll be knocked over, landing squarely on your left leg, and rip up your hand on a nearby concrete wall. Waking up on the ground after a few seconds, you'll have that familiar stunned, echo-y feeling.

A similar scene will reoccur a week later. *Yes*, three mild concussions in the space of two weeks. Not good. But that's what it will take for you to pay attention, to hear the Universe calling.

At this point in your life, you are a whirling dervish of entrepreneurship, creating massive plans, working through the night to craft the perfect copy, training for an Ironman, burning every candle at both ends. You cannot give yourself permission to slow down. Slowing down – in your mind – means failure, stagnation, money left on the table. You will not just *slow down*. So, the Universe steps in. Well, it steps in three times to be exact (you're stubborn). Taking that break will make a huge difference in how you approach your life. What would have happened if you'd listened to that first call to action (or, er, inaction)? What

51

if, after that first fall, you thought, *I'll give myself a chance to heal, to step back and slow down*. Who knows what would have happened if you had kept pushing yourself after that third fall?

The Universe is patient but relentless. She will keep offering you chances to take heed of her warnings and calls. When you don't hear, or ignore the signs, she takes it to the next level.

Do yourself a favor and start listening the first time. You can't outlast the Universe. She always wins.

Life Lesson Challenges
- How does this concept of Universe/Source/God show up in your life?
- When have you felt this existential unsettling? What happened?
- What did you do with this 'call'?
- If you've overlooked these calls in the past, what happened? Why did it feel easier to disregard them?

LIFE LESSON 10

I Wish I Knew the Universe
Has My Back

've never really thought of myself as a religious person. I always envied people of deep faith. Most of them never really seemed to sweat the small stuff. They would say things like: *God will take care of me. God's in my corner.* I was like, "Huh?" I didn't get the trust and belief these folks had for an omnipotent invisible force. Until I did. Until I understood that they were also trusting themselves as much as they were trusting God, because they were inextricably intertwined with God. This is my experience of accepting and leaning into trust in a Universal force, knowing that it's working in my favor. Even (read: especially) if it's not clear at the time how a particular event or decision is serving my greater good. Once you truly believe that the Universe (or

God, Source, the Great Mystery, whichever resonates most) has your back, it's the most tremendous sense of freedom.

🍍 🍍 🍍 🍍 🍍 🍍

Dear Lisa,

One Friday morning, years from now, you'll wake up with a migraine.

That, in and of itself, may not seem significant, but you won't have had a migraine for the better part of a decade. And, it'll happen right when you'll be in the middle of a lot of heavy soul-lifting work, really trying to blow the doors off your new soul-centered business.

That morning, you'll have an appointment on the calendar that will require a 90-minute drive each way. The thought of getting in the car with your head pounding will not, to say the least, be appealing. The shame tape around *responsibility* will start playing in your (pounding) head: *You always quit things. You never show up on time. You're a loser. They'll hate you.*

You've come to realize by now that physical symptoms like the migraine and a handful of others (irritability, aching joints, feeling antsy and tired at the same time) are your somatic red flags telling you that something big is about to happen. It's when your spirit, your Soul, is getting ready to leap the void between the ego-driven human existence and tap into the Universal wellspring of ideas, creativity, and insights.

It's taken you years to figure out this pattern of physical discomfort, which is followed by an emotional/spiritual breakthrough because it is so easy to ascribe the feelings to something else: flu, over-training, bad night of sleep. Or just *life*, right? And, thanks to the duality we've been talking about for several lessons now, you can have flu-like symptoms and not be on the verge of spiritual breakthrough; or you can experience both.

Why is it necessary to have these moments of next-level spiritual awareness? Because this is truly where the magic happens. When we allow ourselves to crack open the barriers we've spent a lifetime creating around awareness, insight, and Universal connection, intense waves of insight flow out.

And, if we are still learning to harness and swim in that potent current of energy, our bodies may feel out of alignment; we may sense our appetite change or feel antsy without cause (like you're over-caffeinated without having drank coffee), or some people may actually feel ill. To you, if often feels like water threatening to spill over a dam if the valves aren't opened to relieve the pressure. A sense of ever-mounting pressure and dis-ease.

You'll physically manifest this dam-spilling warning as migraines and malaise. So, on that Friday morning you'll choose to cancel your appointments, stock up on some *soul supplies* like healthy snacks, kombucha, soup, tea, and, of course, chocolate, and hunker down to wait for whatever the Universe has in store for you. You'll wait for the valves to open so that all the energy and insight can pour out.

At this point in your journey, you'll be debating whether or not to focus full-time on your coaching practice and leave behind the *security* of full-time employment. You'll feel very stuck about it. To pass the time, and keep your consciousness open to the shift, you'll wander around the house, cleaning here and there, folding laundry. No music, no TV. No sensory distractions.

About halfway through the day, you'll sit down to write an email to a friend and find that a conversation has started in your head between you and your Higher Self/Universe.

Not knowing what to do, you'll ignore it at first, taking refuge in normal daily tasks. Feeling increasingly restless, you'll call the dogs and walk out into the backyard, the late afternoon sun setting over the valley and mountains around you. Sitting on a favorite perch, you'll immediately feel calmer. This is where you're supposed to be for whatever is about to happen. And then the voice in your head will come back, insistently. Frustrated, you'll finally start talking back.

I'm only sharing a portion of the conversation as these are very intimate and powerful moments. And, I want you to experience it fully for yourself when the time is right.

YOU: I'm lost, I don't know where to go from here...

UNIVERSE: No, you're not lost. That's not what you're feeling. Try again.

YOU: Maybe...scared?

UNIVERSE: Nope. NEXT.

YOU: Okay, fine, dammit. I know what I'm supposed to do and, if I'm honest, how to do it. But...I don't know what it will cost me. What if the cost is too high?

UNIVERSE: What cost is too high?

YOU: Losing my partner, losing my dogs, losing my home, losing who I think I'm supposed to be...

UNIVERSE: Are those things supporting you or giving you an excuse to walk away from your Truth? Are they a foundation or a crutch?

YOU: Maybe...both?

UNIVERSE: How true is it that you will lose those things when you follow your path? How true is it that if those things disappeared your path would change?

YOU: I don't know if it's true or not. It feels like a possibility that following my path will alienate my partner and I could lose this version of my life.

UNIVERSE: What other possibilities exist? What if letting go of the *attachment* to all of those things brought you exactly what you walked away from? What if that's the secret piece of information you've been missing?

YOU: Right, okay, I get it. If I let go of the attachment, if I focus exclusively on following my calling and your dream, they could grow with me. I could bring them along on my journey. We could buy a different house. We could move to a place we really love. We could leave behind the jobs, the debts, and the things that burden us. We could grow together. And, if we don't, then maybe we weren't supposed to.

UNIVERSE: Who wouldn't want that?

YOU: But I can't control that; the outcome isn't certain.

UNIVERSE: What is certain?

YOU: That my human existence is finite. That I have a calling. That I am capable of love and being loved. I am lovable. That I *am*. I exist.

UNIVERSE: So, what will it *really* cost you to follow your path, your calling? What will it cost you to walk away, again, from your potential?

YOU: Nothing. And everything. I can't live in limbo anymore. I either decide to play all-in or I retire from the game. Both are open to me. I have to decide which one I choose. Staying in limbo is like high-altitude climbing...I can only stay there for so long because I'm dying the whole time.

UNIVERSE: Sounds terrible. Who would choose that?

YOU: No one. I'm not choosing to be there; I just am here.

UNIVERSE: Bullshit. You're choosing to stay in limbo because you want to have your cake and eat it, too. You can't. It's an illusion that will bury you. Decide. Now.

YOU: If nothing is certain, if there are no guarantees, why not live the dream? Why not follow it? I could wake up tomorrow and everything in my world could be gone. Would that change my calling or strengthen it? I feel like I'm using my partner and our financial commitments as an excuse to avoid the hard work of becoming who I'm meant to be.

UNIVERSE: So, back to the question you wouldn't answer...what are you choosing to do? Play big, or not play?

YOU: I want to play. I want to live that life. I want to feel that bliss. But...I have to *not* want it, right? I have to be detached from the outcome.

UNIVERSE: From the outcome, yes, but not from the experience. We only have rights to the labor itself, not the fruits of our labor. Playing all-in means: you create your ass off, in bliss, in flow, following your intuition. It doesn't mean that you just sit around and wait for your dream life to show up – that's not detached involvement, that's avoidance and complacency.

YOU: So, how do I start? How do I start playing all-in?

UNIVERSE: You know.

YOU: Why would I ask if I already knew the answer?

UNIVERSE: Because you don't want to *hear* the answer. You want to reserve the right to be pissed off if it doesn't show up immediately, if there isn't instant gratification.

YOU: Right. Because then I have someone to blame besides myself.

UNIVERSE: You need to decide now, not because I'm telling you to, but because I can see what you can't. That you're sitting on the edge of a cliff and the longer you wait, the more risk you run of that cliff crumbling, of falling. So, what's it gonna be?

[long pause, crying]

YOU: I'm in. All in.

UNIVERSE: I love you. I won't let you fall.

This conversation will happen in your mind, but you'll hear the voice as clearly as if someone were standing next you. The memory will remain so crystal-clear and powerful that even now as I share these words with you, I zoom back to that moment. I can see you in my mind's eyes.

You'll be sitting outside in our backyard. The February sun is setting; the air cooling rapidly.

You will feel the rough concrete step you were sitting on digging into the back of your legs. The wind whipping up the hill, pushing your hair back and forth across your face. The dogs running back and forth across the hillside beneath you.

The goosebumps quivering all over your body have nothing to do with the gathering cold.

And you'll know.

You'll *know*, like I knew.

You're not alone. You'll have someone to talk to; someone who is rooting for you all the time. Someone who will guide you, who will tell you not what you want to hear but what you *need* to hear. The Universe has your back and she won't let you fail.

Life Lesson Challenges

- What connections and conversations do you have with the Universe/God/Source? If none, what gets in your way?
- When do those conversations happen? What are the telltale signs that a conversation or a divine download might be waiting for you (e.g., migraine, malaise)?
- If you haven't had a similar experience, what might it look like to have one?
- What would change in your life if you had this belief that the Universe has your back?
- What action would you take in your life, if you had this deep trust?

LIFE LESSON 11

I Wish I Knew How to Trust
My Triggers

get that this chapter title may seem, at best, crazy and, at worse, dangerous. To be clear, I'm not suggesting you *exacerbate* your triggers. I believe that our triggers are crucially important data points – spiritual breadcrumbs, if you will, that act like a GPS for your self-development work. Because where there are triggers, there is shame. Simply put, shame is the intense feeling that we are unworthy of love and belonging, due to an inherent flaw in our nature. This is also an area where I'll strongly encourage you to speak with a mental health professional and/or coach. Having someone guide you through this process can be extremely helpful. I not an expert on shame, as a concept. I am, however, an expert in my own triggers and the shaming events that created them. I refer to the self-narrative results and reinforcing those shaming events as *shame tapes*. As in, the tapes or self-talk I play in my head when experiencing shame. I use the terms *shame tapes* and *gremlins* interchangeably. For more information on shame, I refer you to anything and everything written, recorded, published, posted or tweeted by Dr. Brené Brown (see the Additional Resources section for suggested reading).

🌵 🌵 🌵 🌵 🌵 🌵

Dear Lisa,

One of the most damaging triggers you'll deal with since childhood is the *patronization* trigger connected to your self-narrative (i.e., shame tape) of not being smart enough. I know you know how this shame tape was formed.

You were in ninth grade. Your class was learning about chemistry of ions and salts. You had a homework assignment to identify the salts in our houses and bring a list to school the next day.

The teacher called on students to share what they'd found. When it's your turn, you'll be excited to share something that the others had not – you'll feel pride in your intellect – and are bursting to tell, waiting for the teacher's approval.

You'll stand up and announce that you've observed calcium carbonate around your shower faucet. In your excitement, you'll mispronounced it as, "calcium bicarbonate." A simple mistake, right?

The teacher will correct you, make a joke at your expense (something about having baking powder in our water, which I'll note is actually *sodium* bicarbonate), and say to you, "*You're not as smart as you think you are.*" The class jeer and you'll sit down, numb, ears burning, throat closed, heart racing and thumping in your chest (all physical symptoms of trauma, by the way).

Up until that day, you'll really enjoy the teacher and the class. I don't know why he says what he does, why he'll feel the need to mock you that day; you'll never ask. What you'll feel in that moment is not guilt or embarrassment about the mistake you made.

Instead, because your ego was proud of your intellect before his comment, you'll experience this as shame rather than embarrassment. This event will wound you at a very deep, soul-level. You've already been subject to teasing and bullying earlier in childhood so it's possible that this conditioning will lower your barrier to experiencing shame.

Other people might laugh it off, feel a flutter of embarrassment or nothing at all. You'll create a shame tape that plays loudly for the next two decades. The *you're not smart enough* gremlin will drive many choices you'll make over years. That single moment will change the course of your life.

You'll hear that shame tape play in your head every time you're handed back a graded assignment in high school. *Look at that crappy grade, you're not as smart as you think you are,* will echo in your head. Even when you get an A, you'll beat yourself up for not getting an A+ or extra credit. You'll always find something to berate yourself about.

Every time you'll debate something with your siblings, you'll hear that gremlin pipe up. *Don't bother having an opinion, you're not as smart as you think you are*.

Every piece of feedback, every grammar correction, every terse email, every question from your thesis advisors: *you're not as smart as you think you are*. Translation: *you're stupid. You're not enough*.

So, you'll begin to make choices that will *prove* to the world that you're smart. (Side note—trying to silence shame tapes with external validation is like running up a down escalator; you'll never arrive, and you'll be completely drained in the attempt.)

You'll think: *if I go to graduate school or medical school, there's no way the world will see me as stupid*. Instant credibility, right?

You'll study for the MCAT and take pre-med courses in college, including two rounds of organic chemistry (holy crap, will that be painful!). You'll get your MCAT results back and your scores won't be high enough to get into med school (sorry about that). It'll be a traumatic double-punch of disappointment: first, you won't be getting the M.D. badge of smartness; and second, the low MCAT scores will confirm the shame tape that you are indeed stupid.

You are, however, a gifted problem solver and the motivation to disprove your shame tape will be strong. After a brief detour working several jobs at a Tupelo, Mississippi hospital, you'll apply and get accepted into a doctoral program at the University of North Carolina at Chapel Hill.

Acceptance into a prestigious university and the ability to become a doctor – albeit a PhD – should feel like a win, right? At that point, this tape is so embedded in your psyche that you'll rationalize this grad school opportunity as a pathetic compromise for not getting into med school. You'll deny your ego any pride around obtaining a perfect score on the GRE analytical portion, the shame tape telling you that it was an easier test than the MCAT (to be fair, there are fewer sections in the GRE and thankfully no organic chemistry).

Is this you complaining about having the opportunity? No.

Are you upset that you got a PhD instead of an MD? No, of course not.

You'll be proud of your accomplishments and that degree will open many professional doors. But, looking back, I realize that my (your) intentions were much more about silencing shame than pursuing a dream.

By uncovering the shame tape that drives your insecurities around your intellect (both how you see it and how others view you) and knowing that you often seek culturally-accepted credentials linked with intelligence (graduate degrees, higher education, etc.), this will give you powerful tools to shred that shame tape.

This uncovering takes place when you confront those destructive self-narratives. Look gremlins right in the eye and *get curious*. Ask yourself: why is this coming up for me now? Where did this belief come from? How do I want to show up?

By doing this work, leaning into your triggers – trusting that they have something important to tell you - rather than trying to silence them, you'll uncover all the ways those shame tapes limit you. You'll learn how to identify the physical symptoms associated with shame tape activation (hint – they are are the same feelings you experience during the initiating event: flushed face, heart racing, numbing sensation).

You'll learn how to gut check that shameful self-narrative, asking yourself questions: *How true is it that you're stupid? You're letting this person trigger you. What else could be going on other than them believing you're stupid? How do you want to show up right now?*

It will be this process – clunky at first, but eventually habitual – that will finally quiet this particular gremlin. It doesn't mean the wheels on the shame tape machine can't and won't start again, but you've found a powerful weapon in your war on shame.

It's amazing how profoundly shame events usurp our rational mind's drive to make choices in our best interests. On tough days – days when you're not taking care of yourself the way you need to – you'll still hear the faint but familiar chords of this tape playing in your head.

Leaning into the trigger and staying curious about why you feel that way will be the first step. Staying judgment free, especially free of self-judgement, is critical. Identifying questions that will help you, in the heat of the moment, and debunk the destructive self-narrative, is the final piece of the puzzle.

Shame requires constant vigilance.

Life Lesson Challenges
- How familiar are you with your triggers and your gremlins?
- What does it feel like when you're triggered? What physical feelings happen when you experience shame?
- What actions do you take as a result of those shame tapes being triggered?
- How would your life change if you saw triggers as data points rather than obstacles?

LIFE LESSON 12

I Wish I Knew How Not to
Should on Myself

Should-ing is all about seeking external validation for your beliefs, actions, and presence. When we *should* on ourselves, we are most often attempting to be accepted by or approved of by others. That's a race that no one wins. We shame ourselves into changing to please other people, who are very often not pleased, and the exhausting, soul-destroying cycle starts all over again. Only when we make changes and take action driven by our internal compass do we find that long-sought fulfillment. In other words, please yourself not others. Make yourself proud.

🍍 🍍 🍍 🍍 🍍 🍍

Dear Lisa,

There will be a point in your journey where you realize that you've broken down enough barriers – not all of them, that's the work of a lifetime – to start deepening your self-awareness and conscious living. Before this point, any attempt to do that would have been met with significant resistance, rumination, and swirl. You just weren't ready.

What does that realization feel like? It'll feel like surrender and trust; like being ready and being scared at the same time. It'll feel like swimming in deep ocean water for the first time. Blissful and scary.

It feels like:
- you're gonna sit on this f-ing chair and figure out what's going on with you – this is very important to you, not matter how afraid you are of the answers,
- you've had it with feeling this way, you want to change,
- you're ready to seek solutions,
- you know there's something else for you to do/offer/ provide to this world, even if you don't know what that something else is.

It does NOT feel like:
- you *should* get your sh*t together, so your spouse/ parent/sibling stops yelling at you,
- you *should* lose ten pounds because you are too fat, so that people stop judging you,

- you *should* get a higher paying job, so people start respecting you,
- you *should* do X, so that Y happens.

See the pattern? Change that comes from within you is transformative. Change that is motivated purely by other's opinions of you or to avoid external conflict is typically driven by shame, fear, and/or self-loathing (or all of the above). What's the easiest way to spot this externally-motivated pressure to change?

One word: *should*. When you start *should-ing* all over yourself, nothing good comes from it.

The best way to make self-transformation stick is to make you, yourself, the only impetus of change *and* the sole beneficiary of said change.

Otherwise, the cycle of dissatisfaction-change-dissatisfaction will keep replaying itself.

Because, as I've shared with you already, when the Universe doesn't get what she wants, she'll keep trying to get your attention.

Life Lesson Challenges
- Do you catch yourself *shoulding* about events or choices? Why, or why not?
- What does *shoulding* on yourself cost you?
- What would change in your life, if you replaced *should* with want or need?
- How does external pressure (peer pressure, society, family) impact your decision-making?

LIFE LESSON 13

I Wish I Knew How to Embrace
My Spirituality

When I was about ten years old, I started to really question the teachings of the Catholic church. I remember sitting in Sunday mass, inhaling the thick smell of incense and old paper, half-listening to the sermon. I kept thinking, *Why? Why does he (the Reverend) get to tell me what to do? How does he know me better than I do? What gives him the right to do that?* I lost the taste for organized religion; more than that, I actively pushed away and ridiculed notions of belonging to a faith community. I realize now that I did that from a place of fear and judgement. At the time, I thought I was choosing freedom and self-determination. What I was really choosing was isolationism. I didn't really experience true freedom until I learned how to surrender control to the Universe, to live

71

in alignment with my values, follow my intuition, and tap into the highest levels of energy. I came back to my spirituality and though it still doesn't align with a specific faith, I have compassion for my ten-year-old self. She just wanted to know she could still be herself and connect with someone beyond herself. For me the term *Universe* resonates; for others, they use terms like God, Source or the Great Mystery, among others. In my opinion, the descriptor is less important than the belief in the existence of a force greater than us.

*   *   *   *   *   *

Dear Lisa,

You knew this was going to be part of the journey, right? You'd make it this far into the book and – wham – I'd hit you with the *woo-woo*. I'd start inviting you to buy crystals, and drink colonics, or book a sweat bath so you could get in touch with the mystics.

Sure, do those things. Do *all* those things, do *everything* that puts you in touch with your soul.

Connect to Source. The Universe. Your Higher Self. God. Divinity.

Whatever word you use to describe the invisible, potent, omnipotent force that unites us all, that's what you're gonna tap into.

I know you never really understood or felt bought into all the rituals of modern Catholicism (it's okay to admit that!). You loved the church with its strange aroma of wood polish, old books, and incense. You loved the stained glass. All the kneeling and standing and sitting seemed a little pointless. In your mind, the Bible is really just another exotic story, a history of a people, not a rulebook to follow.

You won't understand how a book written by men meant there was a God somewhere controlling things. It would be like the world being controlled by the characters in one of your other books. As if someone called Harry Potter could actually be the Universal puppet master? (Trust me, this Harry Potter fellow is someone you'll get to know pretty well).

My invitation to you is: set aside the bitterness and judgement around your experience with Catholicism. Explore the possibility that there is a great force at work in the world. Read books that explore spirituality. When you feel the inevitable judgement rise up, ask yourself why? Why the urge to belittle?

I want to tell you that spirituality is everywhere, in everything. Walking in the woods, reading in your favorite recliner, playing with the dogs. In all things, in everything there is a purpose and an existential hand steering the ship. The sooner you can let the Universe steer, the sooner you can stop wasting energy trying to engineer outcomes.

Embracing your spirituality will bring a deep sense of peace. And, yes, I'm gonna use an f-word here: *faith*. I invite you to cultivate faith that the Universe has your back, it is working for your benefit at all times, and will not let you down.

I like to think of the Universe as the safety net beneath us as we walk the tightrope of life. We may not see it or connect with it consciously at every moment, but it's there just the same, ready to catch us if we fall.

Life Lesson Challenges
- Do you consider yourself a spiritual person? Why or why not?
- What does *spirituality* mean to you?
- If you've resisted identifying as a spiritual person, why is that? What are the barriers?
- How do you embrace spirituality in your life? How does this serve you?

LIFE LESSON 14

I Wish I Knew I Would
Outgrow People

To be clear, I don't view this lesson as an excuse to treat people poorly, be disrespectful or ghost folks in (or out) your life. Quite the opposite. We're all running our own race, as it were, so don't blame people for having a different pace than you. And don't chastise yourself for not holding yourself back for someone that isn't ready to accelerate. For me, this reality means that I've walked away from relationships that I've held dear. Or taken breaks from those relationships. I made those decisions because I knew that it would cost me too much to stay connected with those people at that point in my journey (and in their journey). I wrestled with a *you're so selfish* gremlin for a while before making those decisions. I had to have faith that if I was meant to re-connect with that person, it would happen. If not, I had to be okay with that reality. It took some deep soul-searching and self-scrutiny to discern why I was feeling the intuitive nudge to walk away. Only when I could definitely say that my intention behind this departure fed my growth, and was not based on fear, did I make that tough decision. And, I did my best to explain that with empathy and clarity. I don't know if I succeeded, but I've accepted that the decision was for me, not against anyone.

❦ ❦ ❦ ❦ ❦ ❦

Dear Lisa,

This is gonna be a tough one. This lesson is all about accepting that, as you continue your journey of self-awareness and self-actualization, there are some relationships that you will not keep up. This is not something to blame people for; rather something to acknowledge, accept, and move on from. You will be the recipient of this *outgrowth* or you will experience outgrowing others.

There are only two things that you can be sure of in this life: you *exist*, and you *experience*. Everything else is mutable, changeable, and out of your direct control.

Let things enter your life and leave it when it feels right to you, not when it feels right for other people. Don't *should* yourself into relationships, behaviors, and responsibilities.

We know you don't enter into friendships and relationships easily. As you walk through this journey, you'll resist letting go of these connections from a place of deep scarcity. You won't want to piss anyone off, or hurt them, or feel as though you're condemning yourself to a lonely existence (even when being alone is *exactly* what you want at times).

The simple fact is, not everyone in your life will be with you for the long haul. That may mean family; it will certainly mean friends, lovers, spouses, and pets. This is the natural cycle of life. This is the way it's supposed to happen. You haven't done anything wrong and there isn't anything wrong with you. Every experience has a life span – even your human experience does – and resisting those natural endings will lead to unnecessary suffering. The resistance becomes a barrier in and of itself. It makes every minute, every choice more difficult. Wishing things were different, wishing people would understand you better, wishing you could change someone, are all signs of this resistance.

The thing to realize, here, is that you are exploring new facets of your existence. As you walk through this journey, *you* will change. You'll change how you think, how you feel, what you drink, what you eat. That is how *your* journey proceeds.

However, everyone in your life will not be on the same journey and expecting them to be in lockstep with you will cause heartache and frustration. Many people in your life – friends, colleagues, family – will tell you that you've lost your mind, that you are chasing some unrealistic vision of your life. They'll tell you that you're destroying your life. That you're selfish. That you're deluded. That you are doomed to failure.

Let them say what they need to say. Listen objectively, without letting their words imprint on your heart or soul. Express gratitude, when you can, that they cared enough about you to share these thoughts. And, then, most importantly, let all those words go. Release them. As well-meaning as their advice might be, if it doesn't resonate with you and support your evolution don't act on it.

The most acute suffering is likely to come when you outgrow relationships with people that have been a significant figure in your life, up until now. These people may truly love you; they may also be benefitting from your willingness to put yourself last, to serve their needs first, to subsume your personality to match theirs. Letting go of these relationships will feel more than shooting Class IV rapids than watching the flow of a peaceful river. Hang in there. Stay strong and resolute. Understand that this separation challenges their ego – their sense of self – and egos don't like to be challenged.

When you reach one of these crossroads, lean into your self-awareness and treat them (and yourself) with grace and empathy. Be kind to yourself. *Cry* when you need to. *Laugh* when you need to. Make space in your life to feel what you need to feel. It may feel like a piece of your soul is being ripped away but, really, you're removing old fences. And, just think about the possibilities you're creating for yourself by letting these people and things gently move on from your life.

It will hurt, but the hurt will pass, if you let it bloom rather than resist it. Let them go. Let them run their own race.

Be strong, my love. This too will pass.

Life Lesson Challenges
- How do you know when something in your life no longer matches where you are in your journey?
- What relationships, behaviors, or things have you been holding on to longer then their natural life span?
- How would it feel to let those relationships, behaviors, or things go? What would change in your life?

LIFE LESSON 15

I Wish I Knew How to Call Myself on My Bullsh*t

We all throw up this bulls*t screen as a defensive move. Having the wherewithal to call yourself on this instinct is an invaluable skill to cultivate on anyone's journey of self-awareness. Why? Because it keeps you from spending precious time and energy ruminating, rehashing, procrastinating. It also helps to have a tribe that you trust to call you on bullsh*t with empathy and love. This helps you see it modeled in a supportive environment. Start applying those skills on yourself. Always with empathy and self-love. Always with an intention of change for the better, not punishment.

❦ ❦ ❦ ❦ ❦ ❦ ❦

Dear Lisa,

We all put up layers of excuses and rationalization when faced with vulnerability. It's a normal, human reaction. And, in truth, putting something off for a few hours or days, isn't a huge problem.

It is a problem when you continually get in your own way, avoiding actions you know would benefit you and further your journey.

Here's where your wit and analytical mind comes in handy.

Start calling yourself out on this bullsh*t. When you start making excuses for why you can't go to a meeting or keep an appointment, literally say to yourself, "Nope, I call b.s."

Ask yourself, *what's going on? Why am I afraid? Why am I feeling anxious?* Don't let yourself off the hook, just like you wouldn't have let other folks off the hook if they short-changed your life experience. Be ruthless, but kind. (Yes, you can be ruthless and kind at the same time!)

I'm getting the feeling that you want an example.

At one point in your life, you'll be a triathlete (I know you doubt me, but it's true). Pool swims will be a weekly occurrence. You will also gain more than a few pounds during one off-season and find yourself unable to face putting on a swimsuit and walking the fifteen feet from the locker room to the side of the pool in your suit. You'll have an anxiety attack every time you contemplate going to the pool. You'll keep making excuses for why you can't go swimming: too hot, too cold, too busy, too tired. Then one day, you'll get fed up with the plan-commit-back-out cycle and get really angry. You'll stand in your office crying, so frustrated that one part of your brain is saying, *go swimming, go swimming, go swimming,* while the other part of your brain is saying, *don't do it, you're too fat. They'll laugh at you, they'll shame you.*

When you've learned to call yourself on this b.s., you'll stop, sit down on the floor and start asking yourself questions. *Why do I think this? Why am I procrastinating? Where is all this coming from?*

This simple act of calling yourself on the excuse b.s., will lead to a detour into body image coaching. NOT how you thought it would go. It will lead to you realizing that you've been bullying yourself about your body and your physical appearance for years (sound familiar?). This self-bullying will keep you from experiencing things in your journey; there's nothing to regret, just an opportunity for learning the power of self-awareness.

When you start calling yourself on this rationalization and procrastination, you'll nearly always find a fear lurking around. This is totally normal and perfectly understandable. Dig into this fear. Find out what you're really afraid of and ask yourself how this fear is holding you back. Chances are, it's keeping you playing small.

So, when you can conjure up dozens of excuses for NOT doing something, being somewhere, talking to someone, taking an important decision, do yourself a favor: call b.s on yourself. Lovingly. With the intent to help, not shame.

It'll feel *really* uncomfortable. Do it anyway. Trust me on this one.

Life Lesson Challenges
- When do you catch yourself rationalizing away showing up in your life?
- When and how often are you caught in this plan-commit-back out cycle?

- How would it feel to call b.s. on yourself when you feel the landslide of excuses coming on?
- What do you think is the underlying fear or motivator for avoiding these situations, people, or actions?

LIFE LESSON 16

I Wish I Knew How to Cultivate Gratitude

There is a school of thought that suggests that people who consistently practice gratitude have a fundamentally different life experience than those who don't. They appear to be more resilient, more fulfilled, more capable of navigating life changes. How do they do this? They have some non-negotiable daily ritual that involves expressing gratitude, often including (ahem) journaling. I wish I knew about this years ago. It's really revolutionized the way I handle adversity (is it even adversity, if you're grateful for that experience?) and my ability to truly experience joy. I invite you to incorporate a specific gratitude practice into your day, whatever works for you.

🌵 🌵 🌵 🌵 🌵 🌵

Dear Lisa,

At this point in your life, skepticism rules your decision-making more than openness. That's completely understandable and anyone in your shoes, given your life experiences, would feel the same.

If you remember nothing from my attempt to give you the key to future happiness and fulfillment, remember the power of gratitude.

At this point in your journey, the mere whiff of anything New Age will make you gag. You'll run away from those people talking about sound healing and yoga. (Note—the yoga thing will *really* take off. I'd recommend buying stock in something called Lululemon. Yes, that's the name of an *actual* company).

You don't need to drop your analytical veil of science and fact. Just start with something really simple. Start writing down, every day, three things you're grateful for in your life. Just three things. You can do that, right? It needs to happen every day.

I'm sensing resistance.

Don't take my word for it. Here's are some benefits of a daily gratitude practice, based on *scientific* research (see what I did there):

- Gratitude increases happiness and decreases depressive symptoms.[1]
- Gratitude discourages materialism and envy, while encouraging generosity.[2]
- Gratitude promotes pro-social behavior and the instinct to help others[3]

1 Seligman M et al., 2005. *American Psychologist*, 60(5): 410-421. *Link.*
2 McCullough ME et al., 2002. *Journal of Personality and Social Psychology*, 82(1): 112-127. *Link.*
3 McCullough ME et al., 2001. Psychological Bulletin, 127(2): 249-266. *https://nccih.nih.gov/health/meditation/overview.htm*

An *attitude* of gratitude is a great first step, but a gratitude *practice* (emphasis on the practice) is light years better. This doesn't have to require a big effort; in fact, *simpler is better*.

1. Grab a notebook (I know you have an office supplies addiction so don't pretend you can't find something to write on!).
2. Number a list 1 through 3.
3. Write down three things you're grateful for in your life. Be as specific as possible.
4. Write an appointment down in your planner for every day at 4 pm. (Note—later, you'll set an alarm for this on your iPhone. I know you don't know what that is. Again, might be worth buying stock in a company called Apple. Yes, that's the name of an actual company).

Do this every day and you'll start to notice changes in your life.

This simple practice will change how you view your life, how you interact with others. That feeling of dread and heaviness will gradually lift.

This isn't about instant gratification; it's about ingraining a new, very important habit that will cultivate happiness and fulfillment in your life.

Life Lesson Challenges

*   What is your current approach to cultivating gratitude?
*   If you don't currently have a daily gratitude practice, what is getting in the way?
*   What would a daily gratitude practice look like?
*   If you are investing time in a daily gratitude practice now, how could this deepen? How could you take it to the next level?

LIFE LESSON 17

I Wish I Knew to Meditate Every Day

'm certainly not an expert on meditation, in the sense that I'm a practitioner not an instructor. There are many free resources these days - guided meditations, music, scripts, apps – I invite you to explore how to integrate meditation into your daily routine. There's a lot of spiritual materialism and elitism out there today. You don't really need special equipment. You don't really need a fancy app. You only need a willingness to try. Start experimenting with a meditation practice that feels right for you no matter what anyone else is doing. Try a five-minute meditation. Or even just start with three deep breaths, eyes closed, feet resting on the ground. Start simple. Simple is good.

Dear Lisa,

I know. I know. Meditation is way outside your comfort zone.

It's hard for you to imagine sitting still for one minute, let alone ten. An hour of meditation sounds like an eternity. I get it.

Like the gratitude practice, including meditation in your daily routine now will pay huge dividends later in life.

Again, this isn't just my opinion. There will be a lot of research compiled by everyone from faith healers to neurobiologists, discussing the many benefits of meditation and a technique called *mindfulness*.

Meditation is a practice where an individual uses a technique – such as mindfulness, or focusing their mind on a particular object, thought or activity – to train attention and awareness, and achieve a mentally clear and emotionally calm and stable state. Meditation has been practiced for centuries, often as part of a religious or spiritual belief pattern, as a path towards enlightenment and self-realization.

I know. More psychobabble, New Age sh*t. Deep breath.

Scientists and clinicians will accumulate thousands of data points (including brain scans) suggesting that consistent meditation appears to reduce stress, anxiety, depression, and pain, while increasing peace, contentment, fulfillment.[4] Even if you don't believe in its power, yet, you can't argue with the benefits.

I know you struggle with anxiety and that you try desperately to hide it from everyone. I know that acid thump you feel in your stomach when you think about talking to people or speaking up in front of the class. This will help you calm your mind and feel more in control of...well...everything.

---

4   National Center for Complementary and Integrative Health, "Meditation: In Depth". *https://nccih.nih.gov/health/meditation/overview.htm*

Meditation will help you calm those waves of worry and panic. Your mental clarity and focus will increase. Perhaps, most importantly, you will *feel* calmer and more controlled. You will get off the emotional rollercoaster with its manic highs and suffocating lows. In short, you'll mellow out, but not at the cost of brain power and drive. If anything, you'll be more productive because you won't be injecting energy into constantly controlling your emotions. You'll simply acknowledge, accept, and choose. Meditation will help you access that pattern.

Eventually you'll be able to listen to thousands of meditation scripts with a flick of your finger. On your *phone* (I realize how odd that sounds, bear with me).

For now, try playing your favorite classical or instrumental music. You could also turn on the radio, if you're roommate hasn't stolen it again.

1. Pop in your cassette tape of George Winston's *December.*
2. Put one of the big couch cushions on the floor.
3. Sit cross-legged atop the cushion, rest your hands lightly on your knees, keeping your spine straight.
4. Softly focus your eyes, looking straight ahead (sort of like in organic chemistry class when you start to day dream and everything is visible but kinda fuzzy).
5. Take three deep breaths, in through your nose, out through your mouth, paying close attention to how it feels in your body.
6. Close your eyes and start breathing in and out through your nose normally.
7. Focus on your breath, the feeling of your chest rising and falling and expanding. The feeling of air coursing in and out of your nose.
8. If thoughts appear in your head (which is normal), softly wave them away, mentally (i.e., not with your hand!).

9.   Keep this up for two full songs or tracks on the tape.
10. Then, when the second song ends, slowly blink your eyes open and notice how you feel.

Work up to doing this every day for as many songs as you can. I know it seems simple. I know it's crazy to think that this could create any change whatsoever (except possibly flattening your couch cushions). Looking back, I wish I'd started these practices years ago.

Also, I found out (the hard way) that monk's robes are comfy but optional.

Life Lesson Challenges
*   What does *meditation* mean to you?
*   Do you have a meditation practice? Why or why not?
*   What do you feel are the benefits of meditation, for you?

LIFE LESSON 18

I Wish I Knew How to Rock My Style

Why include this lesson? First, it's funny and I love a good laugh (obviously). Second, there *is* a deeper life lesson here. The lesson revolves around knowing yourself completely, searching for knowledge and expansion, *not* seeking to change your essential nature. All of the above commentary is (hopefully) funny and also illustrates experiments we all undertake to express ourselves. Admittedly, this lesson focuses on a superficial level (and the superficial lessons change as we age), but constantly seeking to redefine my look was more about a deep-rooted dissatisfaction with who I thought I was supposed to be rather than a playful exercise in self-expression.

Dear Lisa,

Look. I'm being your friend here.
Just say no to capri pants.
NOOOO. Leave them on the rack. Trust me.
Walk away.

While we're at it, here are some other questionable fashion choices I invite you to think twice about:
- Don't wear the white studded leather miniskirt. ('Nuff said.)
- That black velvet jumpsuit. (Oh, no, honey. Put it down.)
- White jeans. (Not with your gravitational field, my friend).
- Sweater twin sets. (You are more Joan Jett, less Jackie O).
- Page boy haircuts. (Nyet, comrade.)

I'm saying all of this because I know that constantly seeking a new look is not really about fashion trends. It's about trying to fit in.

I want you to know that you have a style all your own. This goes beyond genres or categories of clothing. It's about owning who you are in each moment and celebrating it. Some days you're a goth chick. Some days you are boho chic. Or rocking a power suit.

The point is, no matter what you're wearing, you are expressing who you are.

You don't have to choose to be one thing or another; you are an unlimited being. So, keep rocking whatever style feels good to you, unapologetically.

Life Lesson Challenges
- How and when does changing your appearance resonate with self-expression?
- When does altering your appearance link back to a desire to change who you are?
- What lessons have you learned about self-expression over the years?
- What does seeking external approval of how you look or act cost you?

LIFE LESSON 19

I Wish I Knew that Loving Myself Really Means Finding True Love

It's taken me four decades to come to terms with the fact I am worthy of love and belonging. And, that loving myself does not detract or prevent me from having loving relationships with others. In fact, quite the opposite. In my experience, once this lesson really sank in for me, all of the relationships in my life deepened and bloomed. So, the thing I was seeking for forty years only really appeared after I let go of the desire to *be loved* and focused on loving myself. Well played, Universe. Well played.

Dear Lisa,

What you didn't know then – but which I know now – is that you can't give people something you don't have. You can't give love until you feel love for yourself, until you have built up enough love capital in your existential bank account to make withdrawals. You'll keep trying to show up and you'll keep over-drafting, getting into spiritual and psychological debt, reinforcing your belief of being less than. Some people may disagree with me and that's fine; I know this to be true for our journey.

There will be days when self-love sounds like a sales pitch for a bubble bath rather than a mantra for inspired, whole-hearted living. Bubble baths are certainly a way to care and show love for yourself. I'm talking about going a few levels deeper than that.

I'm talking about using loving words to speak to yourself, especially during difficult times. I'm talking about being kind and compassionate to yourself when the easiest thing to do is blame yourself for how life seems to be turning out.

It'll feel good to bully yourself somedays. You'll shame yourself when those instincts arise. You confuse self-bullying with motivation some days. "*Get up, lazy,*" you'll shout at yourself. Not jokingly. Not with a twinkle in your eye.

You'll become the stereotypical drill sergeant about *every* aspect of you and your life.

Nothing will be good enough.

Not your grades, your height, your weight, your complexion, your job, your laugh, your smile. You will spend years in this self-demolition mode. And you'll try to pursue relationships during these tough years. When those don't work out, you'll blame and shame yourself, again.

Here's the good news: you *are* that bullying, shaming drill sergeant so *you* can fire them.

You can demote them from that line of service and put them to work helping you figure out what self-love means. You'll experiment with a lot of things to fill that self-love bank account. You'll try massages, pedicures, vitamins, and new books. It'll feel good to be pampered – remember that feeling. And look for ways to deepen it. Go beyond the low hanging fruit.

Here's the reality check: you're gonna have to dig deep on this. For every shaming and blaming comment you've hurled toward yourself, you'll need to identify two or three loving truths about who you are. This is gonna take work. It's gonna take objective thinking and a willingness to be uncomfortable (not your forte, I know). You'll need to stand and look at yourself in the mirror and learn to love what you see. *Love.* Not tolerate or explain away. Not rationalize, or cover up, or avoid what you see. *Love. Appreciation. Gratitude.*

Keep chasing those experiences of self-love. Keep exploring. Be relentless. Little by little, all those tiny points of light – those moments of self-love – will condense into a fire in your soul.

Then, and only then, my love, will you be able to really give love. To truly give and receive love from others in your life. To light their soul-fires. You may have relationships before this point, and you may care deeply for people in your life. This is the point where all those connections begin to deepen and strengthen.

Maintain and expand this self-love by setting boundaries, valuing your opinion, speaking up and sharing your gifts, walking through life with empathy and light. You will blossom and bloom. People will be drawn to you and your reserves of love will flow freely.

You will know true love in a relationship, too. I know you doubt that, and I know, right now, you doubt that you're worthy of love. I know how heartbreaking that is, how it catches in your throat and how many nights you've cried yourself to sleep feeling this emptiness.

Yes, the kind of love they write about in books and movies. And, that person will be with you for your whole life.

She is you and you are her. Choose love.

Life Lesson Challenges
- How do you define self-love?
- How do you cultivate self-love in your life? What's worked for you and what hasn't been so effective?
- What is it costing you to focus on loving others before (or rather than) loving yourself?
- What would it feel like to walk through the world with this well of self-love powering your thoughts, feelings, and actions?
- How did (or would) the relationships with yourself and others change if you felt this strong, inner wealth of self-love?

LIFE LESSON 20

I Wish I Knew How to Ask for Help

I know I'm not alone in struggling with this aspect of the self-actualization journey. I always prided myself on being able to do everything myself. My childhood hero, MacGyver, saved a nuclear power plant in full melt-down with a chocolate bar and a gum wrapper. I mean, come on! If he can do that singled-handedly, I'm not gonna ask for help, right? That kind of thinking painted me into all sorts of existential and operational corners. Ironically, I'm also a person who loves to support others and, ahem, help them. Nowadays, when I feel the urge to turn down help, I remember how good it feels when I'm able to help others. It helps shift that ego-drive pride to gratitude and acceptance. I've gotten better at asking for support when I need, and accepting that this is a normal part of life. It takes a village, after all.

🍍 🍍 🍍 🍍 🍍 🍍

Dear Lisa,

Ever heard of something called a *truthbomb* or it's more intense older sister, the truthb*tch slap?

Okay, good, 'cuz I have one for you.

Here it is…you are not a superhero.

You can't do this alone. You can't do *life* all by yourself.

Yes, I know, I know what you're gonna say. You don't want to *need* people.

Roger, that. Message received.

Get over it (she said with great love and empathy).

At certain times in your life, you will need support more than others. When asking for help, it's very natural to feel vulnerable. It's human nature to want to avoid vulnerability and very difficult for you to admit that you can't take care of everything on your own.

Asking for help allows you to focus your energy on the aspects of life you truly can accomplish alone rather than running yourself ragged.

My invitation to you is to recognize the signs that you need some help, when having another perspective, feedback, or extra set of hands, might ease your path forward.

Here are some guideposts for when to ask for help:

- You've tried everything you can think of and nothing is working, nothing makes it (whatever *it* is) better,
- You spend hours running through the problem in your head, obsessing over it, without seeing any options,
- You can't sleep or aren't hungry because this issue robs you of rest and appetite,

- When you think of this problem, you instantly think of someone in your life that you know might have the answer,
- You can't remember the last time you *didn't* think about this problem or thing.

This isn't about needing people in the sense that you become so enmeshed in their world and their lives that you lose who *you* are. It's not about subsuming your opinion or desires to please someone else. That's not what I'm advocating for here. At all. That's not help. That's co-dependency, and likely just as harmful as trying to go it alone (see *Life Lesson #33*).

This is about being honest with yourself when having help will get you to your goal faster and easier. Who wouldn't want that?

Life Lesson Challenges
- What does help mean to you? What about support? Which of these words resonates most strongly for you?
- When is it most difficult for you to ask for help? When is it easiest to have people help you? What lesson can you learn from these two situations?
- Where in your life are you avoiding asking for help? Why? What's stopping you from reaching out?
- What is not asking for help or support costing you?

LIFE LESSON 21

I Wish I Knew About Numbing and How to Stop Doing It

'm not an expert in the psychology, neurobiology, or sociology of numbing. I am becoming an expert in understanding all the ways I've used numbing in my life to repress emotions and give into my escapism rather than cultivate awareness. I'm not blaming myself or anyone who engages in numbing – this is a human condition – rather, I wish to gently, empathetically, lovingly let my younger self know (and you, my dear reader) what numbing can look and feel like. The pattern is different for everyone. And, as you'll read below, I had many weapons in my numbing arsenal. Intention is what separates a healthy habit from a numbing habit. Learning how to check in myself around intention led to a game-changing self-awareness. I still struggle with numbing these days, especially around food. I try to take a mindful approach to exercise rather than pushing myself to extremes to avoid dealing with self-judgement. I still feel anxious from time to time, but acknowledge and accept it as part of the human experience, rather than an indicator to start numbing and distracting myself from that feeling. Once awareness is in place, change can occur.

* * * * * *

Dear Lisa,

Numbing isn't part of your vocabulary right now, which is totally understandable and makes perfect sense.

So, perhaps a definition is in order. According to experts in the field, numbing consists of behaviors that one uses compulsively and chronically to avoid feeling shame, anxiety or disconnection.

Numbing is a destructive force in your life. We all do it to some degree. It's a normal reaction to vulnerability and shame. But very destructive.

Numbing will become a daily part of your life, triggered by your personal challenges and from absorbing the negativity of people in your life. You are very empathic and will eventually learn how to create energetic boundaries in your life to prevent absorbing the emotional baggage that people (consciously or subconsciously) ask you to carry.

Over the next few years, you will become a worrier. Anxiety driven by the fear of uncertainty – normal human emotions – will become a perpetual way of life. So, you'll do what you need to do to escape.

Some days, the escape will look like busyness. You'll work. *A lot*. And you'll get praised for it and told that you're irreplaceable. So, you'll work harder, following that praise.

Some days, you'll drink. It won't be every night but some nights you will binge, black out and wake up in unfamiliar places. You'll scare yourself and stay away from booze for a few nights or weeks. Then, on really rough days, you'll find yourself alone, at a bar, for hours. Ignoring people who talk to you or, worse, letting them distract you. You'll stumble home on cold winter nights, walking alone, flaunting how much you don't worry about your safety, your façade of invincibility.

Some days, you'll shop. You'll buy things you don't need or don't want, just to have something to do. Your closet will be full and your heart empty. You'll flaunt with financial disaster, distracting yourself even further with these crises.

At one point, you'll use exercise and food (or lack of food) as numbing. You'll push your body hard, really hard; you won't eat. You tell yourself it's healthy to lose weight, to be fit. Inside you won't feel fit or healthy; you'll feel lost and empty. So, you'll numb more.

What I know now, and what I want to share with you, is that you engage in all these numbing behaviors to escape from feeling unworthy. You feel broken and unloveable. A void exists in your soul that cannot be filled, and you will do your best to satisfy that longing for connection and acceptance. This escapism will cost you relationships, safety, health, and financial solvency (hello, crappy credit score). Not to mention all the emotional yo-yo-ing and heartbreak.

You aren't alone in these habits. You will cross paths with other people who numb the same way and you'll convince yourself that you support each other, rather than keep each other bogged down in an emotional blackhole.

What makes this situation even more challenging is that the actions you take to numb are societally acceptable – even, societally *prized*. Exercise, being thin, working hard, buying luxury items, being fun and sociable (a.k.a., drinking a lot).

So, how do you know when you're numbing and when you're not? It's all about how you feel when you're engaging in these behaviors and your intention behind it

When you're in the middle of an activity you feel compelled to do and you don't feel joy, passion or fulfillment, chances are high that you're numbing, not experiencing.

For example, if you're craving chocolate and you find yourself eating chunks of chocolate without tasting them, feeling like there can never be enough chocolate to satisfy you, that's numbing. If, however, you eat those chunks of chocolate slowly, enjoying the flavor, feeling that warmth and joy flood your body, feeling satiety, then it's likely not numbing.

But and this is a big but, the *intention* behind the action is the most important differentiator. If you're seeking an escape, that's numbing.

Explore those intentions. Ask yourself some tough questions:
- Why am I doing _____?
- What do I derive from _____?
- Does _____ fill me with joy, passion, fulfillment?
- Do I feel better after _____ or worse?

If you can't answer these questions, my suggestion is to pause until you can. Take a break from exercise, shopping, drinking booze, and working crazy hours until you *can* answer the questions. Talk to experts. Seek help from qualified healers.

The cost to stop these activities for a few weeks may seem high but the cost of numbing will be much, much higher.

Understanding which vulnerabilities you are avoiding by numbing will be an uncomfortable process. You'll have to dig past the top layers of avoidance and rationalization; you need to understand *why* you are numbing.

That is the key to transforming the way you walk through life—knowing *why* the numbing is happening and making the choice to change your behavior and regaining control of your life.

Life Lesson Challenges

- How does numbing show up in your life? What are your triggers?
- Can you think of two or three activities that you automatically turn to in times of great stress or anxiety?
- What does numbing cost you, in terms of time, energy, or financial resources?
- What drives you to numb? How would you rather show up instead, during those times?

LIFE LESSON 22

I Wish I Knew How Much My Scarcity Mindset Would Control Me

Scarcity in this context is exactly what it sounds like and what I describe below: not enough-ness. You may recognize this theme of not-enough-ness across many areas of life. There are reasons for that. First, I experienced a lot of scarcity, shame, and disconnection in my life. I'm working through that and have made significant progress towards living with a sense of true abundance, no matter what life throws my way. Two, sometimes we, as learners and readers, need to be hit over the head with concepts a few times so they sink in. I'm certainly in that bucket. Scarcity mindset around money was definitely one of the most difficult lessons I learned on this journey.

Dear Lisa,

Scarcity is essentially the belief that everything is limited, from money, to love, to opportunities. Everything in life's inventory could go out of stock at any time. So, if something's presented to you, scarcity mindset says *take it* because it won't come around again. This often leads to overwhelm, over-scheduling, over-committing, and generally feely crappy about all the life decisions you're making.

Scarcity will show up most markedly for you in two places: finances and love.

Money will be a challenge for you (so much so that there's a whole chapter on how to make friends with money! Check out Life Lesson #38).

In your life, you'll alternate between spending lavishly and hoarding money away. Sometimes in the same day. Money will seem, to you, like an enemy to be conquered. There will never seem to be enough money and the pursuit to get more will cloud your decision-making (i.e., taking jobs that don't interest you simply because there's a higher paycheck).

But, more than the operational view of scarcity, the most damaging aspect of this mindset is the anxiety and sense of being confined. *You can't buy this. You can't afford that; it costs too much. Your paycheck is too small. Your bills are too large. There's no way to get more money. It all flows out. It never flows in.*

Life becomes a series of calculations: too much, too little, not enough, not much.

The same goes for you and your mindset around love. You'll fall in love with people and feel loss when they interact with others, as if it subtracts away from your love. This manifests in jealousy, envy, and bitterness. A little nugget of truth that may help here: jealousy works the opposite way you want it to.

You'll push people away by trying to keep them close.

You'll miss out on experiences because of envy or bitterness.

You'll forego pleasure to horde pennies.

You'll make choices that put your happiness, safety, and even survival at risk.

I'm not saying this to hurt you, rather to let you know this is how scarcity plays out. You're not crazy. There's nothing wrong with you. This is how anyone in your situation, with your level of self-awareness would act. When you choose to see lack – lack of love, lack of affection, lack of ownership – that's is exactly what you'll feel and experience.

I also want to say, *you're not alone*. You and I live in a culture of not-enough-ness, even though we're separated in time by decades. People around us are obsessed with obtaining more, achieving more, being more. It's all about *never enough. Never smart enough, never skinny enough, never popular enough, never _____ enough* (insert attribute).

When you live in and act out of this mindset, people and wealth will leave your life, only reinforcing your belief that you're inherently unlovable and bankrupt (spiritually and literally).

I know you're tired of that weight on your soul. None of your numbing strategies are working (remember Life Lesson #21 on *Numbing?*). I know you're tired of feeling that emptiness.

So, what's a person to do?

The way to battle through scarcity is gratitude and self-awareness. Not working harder to make someone love you. Not focusing on possessing a person completely so that they don't have the ability to interact with others. Not focusing on how little you have in terms of resources and finances.

Be grateful for what you have in your life, and the people you have in your life.

Be grateful for the resources you have.

Be aware of all the incredible, unique, powerful gifts you bring to the table.

Be aware of how much money and wealth is all around you.

Realize that scarcity is rooted in *your* feelings of unworthiness; not the world being fair or unfair, fate handing you a good job or a sh*t job, or a romantic partner flirting too much or ignoring you.

If you really feel and believe in your own worthiness none of these actions or thoughts will impact your life. You'll operate from a place of *enough*. I am enough, always and in all ways.

That's your goal. Your goal is to cultivate a sense of deep worthiness. Easy, right?

It's a concept that can be intellectualized, but *living* it is more challenging. Especially when faced with all the ups and downs life throws at you.

This isn't the work of a day or a week.

This is the work of your lifetime. I invite you to start the process as soon as possible.

Life Lesson Challenges
- What does scarcity mean to you?
- How does scarcity show up in your life or your world?
- What experience do you have (or did you used to have!) with jealousy and envy?
- What role does financial scarcity play in your life? How do you work through those feelings and belief?
- How can you cultivate a deep sense of self-worthiness, around both love and money? What would that feel like? What actions would you take?

LIFE LESSON 23

I Wish I Knew How to
Thrive Not Just Strive

Striving, by definition, requires you to make great efforts to achieve or obtain something. Thriving on the other hand, involves flourishing and prospering. Do I think you can strive *and* thrive? Yes, I do (I see you shaking your head). Like so many life lessons in this book, this topic revolves around intention and awareness. If you are putting great effort into something that is smack-dab in your zone of genius, something that fills you with joy, I would argue that this is healthy striving. It sits at the intersection (think, Venn diagram) of strive and thrive. That, in my opinion, is the ultimate sweet spot.

🌵 🌵 🌵 🌵 🌵 🌵

Dear Lisa,

At this time in your life, you'll be all about the striving. That's not a bad thing, per se. In our twenties and thirties, striving is a big part of our experience. When you're that age, you can handle striving. Mostly.

As you age, the striving – constantly forcing and hustling to outpace our fears – is tiring. And, honestly, the things you're striving for also change. Before, you're working to establish who you are, feeding the ego's self-identity, working to determine your rank in the cultural hierarchy. Again, that's pretty normal.

Once you pass a certain point, all that hustling seems like a big chore. And, like a big energy sink. *Why*, you'll ask, *why am I pushing so hard? Why am I hustling every day to prove who and what I am? What's the point?*

Striving will show up in your life most markedly around career and work-a-holic tendencies. Similar to other types of actions motivated by fear, or perfectionist tendencies, your drive to work harder and longer than anyone else is not really about success. You work and over-schedule yourself so that the *crazy-busy* mental track is louder than the *crazy out of touch with my emotions and values* track. Which also links up with Life Lesson #21 around numbing.

As you work around-the-clock, you'll start hearing that inner voice, a compulsion, to slow down, savor, enjoy a bit more of life, live more purposefully.

So, what are you waiting for?

Oh, right. Your job. The attachment to your ego. The reality of all that *free time* to think and confront your emotions. The loss of income. Loss of purpose.

These are all understandable concerns. The longer you put off listening to that voice, the more discontent you'll feel. Prolonging that transition produces some necessary and instructive discomfort.

Thriving means, you'll start following your heart and listening to your soul. Healthy striving means following your heart, listening to your soul, and working your butt off to follow that guidance.

As you walk through your journey, your relationship with striving and thriving will not necessarily be linear or mutually exclusive. You'll toggle between thriving and striving, sometimes hitting the sweet spot. Sometimes, focusing on one over the other. This is absolutely normal and all a part of life's ever-changing cycles. My invitation to you is to be aware of the relative amount of striving and thriving in your life right now and compare that to your optimal ratio.

Life Lesson Challenges
- Where in your life are you striving, tolerating conditions, ignoring that voice in your head?
- What's on your bucket list?
- How would it feel to turn that bucket list into a *f*ck-it* list, as "in, "F*ct-it", I'm doing this?" What would get in your way?
- Not ready to completely stop striving? How can you incorporate more thriving practices (sole purpose, mindful work and rest, etc.)?
- What does striving all the time cost you? How does it interfere with your ability to thrive?
- What is your ideal ratio of strive/thrive right now? What would that ratio look like one year or five years from now?

LIFE LESSON 24

I Wish I Knew How to Discern Where My Responsibility Starts and Ends

One of the biggest revelations I experienced during my coach training was that I (and I alone) am responsible for my emotions. Yup. Seems pretty obvious, doesn't it? Understanding that I could chose to feel differently was like someone handing me the keys to a Formula One race car. Wait, you mean I get to drive *this*? I have access to all that horsepower, seriously? I remember that mind blowing moment when I realized that meant I was the one choosing to feel disgust, fear, anger. I could choose *not* to feel those things, if I wanted to. It also meant, I alone could determine when I would feel happy, satisfied, or joyful. It wasn't just about banishing the Darkness; I also controlled the Light. And, with great power comes great responsibility.

🌵 🌵 🌵 🌵 🌵 🌵

Dear Lisa,

You are only, ever responsible for you. You, and you alone.

Your actions. Your beliefs. Your emotions. Your thoughts.

You cannot take someone else's pain away from them. You cannot help someone when they won't help themselves. You cannot make someone fall in love with you (or out of love with you). You do not have the power to make someone else *happy*.

This is a such an important lesson for you to learn. You were raised to be kind and compassionate. There's nothing wrong with that; nothing at all.

When that kindness and compassion becomes over-taking responsibility, this is a losing proposition. When you start trying to control someone else's emotions (even to *help* them), or feeling like it's your job to make them feel a certain way, then you've entered into a dangerous pattern.

Why *dangerous*?

Because this is an unwinnable war.

You have no way of making someone feel anything. *Anything*.

Over-taking responsibility will always lead to disappointment and self-judgement. You'll blame yourself for not fixing things, for not making something easier for someone you love. You'll blame yourself and carry the burden for things that are so far out of your control, you probably won't believe me if I tell you.

This doesn't make you a bad person; it does make you a tired, over-extended, frustrated, and super apologetic person. Sorry (oops).

Which brings me to a big red flag for over-taking responsibility: those moments when you find yourself apologizing over and over again (there's a whole chapter, Life Lesson #48, on apologizing, too; it's an issue).

Here's an example: Your spouse comes home after a tough day at work, angry and frustrated. He starts venting about it. You sit there, hunched in your chair, listening to the venting, blaming yourself for (somehow) not being able to wave a magic wand and make his day better. You feel responsible for his discomfort; you actually take it into yourself, it becomes *your* discomfort now. All of a sudden, you feel like *your* day was frustrating, even though two seconds ago, you were having a perfectly fine day. You tell yourself that really, truthfully, you are the reason he's upset. Your worthiness is now based on whether or not you can take away his frustration. You try and fail to dispel that discomfort, so you blame yourself. This is how over-taking responsibility will often appear in your world.

So, what to do about it?

First, check in and ask yourself, "What can I *actually* control in this situation? What is *truly* my responsibility?"

Second, once you're crystal clear on what you can control and where your responsibility stops/ends, choose to let that discomfort or guilt transform into something that works for you such as curiosity and empathy.

Third, if you still feel compelled to engage and help dispel someone else's discomfort (from a place of healthy boundaries), ask questions. Ask how you can support them? Perhaps they just need a safe place to vent. Perhaps they would like to brainstorm with you.

If you take this curious approach, they can help steer you towards what works for them.

If you withdraw into your self-blame shell and over-taking vortex, you can't help anyone, least of all yourself.

Life Lesson Challenges
- Where or when in your life do you struggle with knowing what you're responsible for? In what ways do you over-take responsibility for others?
- How does it feel when you over-extend and over-take responsibility for people's emotions or behaviors?
- How could you set boundaries around your responsibility taking?
- How would it feel to approach these situations with curiosity and empathy, rather than self-blame?

LIFE LESSON 25

I Wish I Knew How to Set and Defend Healthy Boundaries

Boundaries can be a divisive word these days. Are we talking about excluding people who challenge you? Are we talking about piling on emotional armor or escapism (i.e., numbing)? Some people prefer the word *standards* rather than boundaries, objecting to the implication that they need to defend themselves against an assault. To each their own, and I invite you to explore this for yourself. For me, boundaries begin with awareness and are built with an intention to protect my energy. Now, if you've just read the chapter on emotional responsibility (Life Lesson #24), you might be thinking if she's in control of her emotions, why does she even need boundaries? Here's why this is true for me. I am very empathic. I love supporting people and when I get into that, "How can I help you?" mode, too deep and without awareness, I become an emotional sponge. I sop up people's fear, anxiety, uncertainty, despair, frustration, anger. I try to carry it for them and by doing so, injure myself. I want to help them climb out of that pit of sh*t (as one of my brilliant fellow coaches, Christina Lord, refers to it) so much, to relieve them of those burdens, that I may switch places with them: pulling them out of the muck and being mired in it myself. Boundaries help me fulfill my love and passion for supporting people through life transitions while maintaining objectivity and without slip-sliding into the sh*t.

🌵 🌵 🌵 🌵 🌵 🌵

Dear Lisa,

So…let me tell you something that might not be a news flash: you're a people pleaser.

Your ability to make people happy is directly tied, in your mind, to your self-worth. Check out *Life Lesson #24* about over-taking responsibility as these are inter-related concepts.

You say, "Yes," to everything. You don't want to disappoint people. You find yourself staring at forty hours of work with only four hours to get it done.

You lose sleep, don't take care of yourself, walk away from happiness so that others aren't put out, so they don't get mad at you, or feel disappointed in you.

Here's the deal. You *do* have a responsibility in this. That responsibility is to yourself. *You.* This sense of needing to make sure everyone else is happy and content relates directly back to scarcity (Life Lesson #22).

This desire to please or relieve suffering will be fueled by worry that if people are angry with you, then they'll leave. You tell yourself that their happiness equals your acceptance and worth. If you don't make them happy, you'll have failed. This is a very normal, fundamental fear and something a lot of people experience: the *fear of rejection.*

Way back in ancient tribal days, rejection meant your survival was uncertain. We're talking literal survival here. Without the tribe, your food source, shelter, and safety were at risk. Survival depended on acceptance and inclusion.

Our species has moved on since those days – although you and I could have a lengthy conversation about whether or not this represents true *progress* in terms of species evolution – but the neurological hard wiring around inclusion and acceptance persists. It would seem that our neurobiology has not yet caught up to our social evolution.

So, when you feel this fear of rejection, your brain isn't really able differentiate between social/ego survival and literal survival. The same chemicals flood your body, you feel the same stress and fear. So, you do what any other human would do in that situation. You do whatever you need to do to ensure you're not voted off the island. When social isolation is at stake, you'll make choices that you can't possibly believe you'd make. You see yourself doing and saying things that are so out of alignment with who you thought you were, that it's more akin to an out-of-body experience.

So, how do you overcome this hard wiring?

It starts, as do so many lessons, with searching inside yourself.

Understand your motivations for helping someone. If service is the intention, then it's not people-pleasing and the survival of your ego isn't at stake. Service is the desire to help someone without seeking any benefit for yourself. People pleasing is not pure service, because you are hoping to get validation of your worthiness by helping someone.

Other examples include:

- Serving with the intention of controlling someone's actions = self-destructive,
- Serving with the intention of avoiding conflict = self-limiting,
- Serving with the intention of self-expression = yes, sharing your gifts!
- Serving with the intention of giving freely of your gifts = constructive!
- Serving with the intention of forcing your opinions on others = losing battle.

Again, it's all about intention behind the action.

Understand which emotions are yours and which are theirs. Leave theirs alone. Acknowledge and support them in naming their feelings, but don't take on their burden. You aren't doing yourself or *them* any favors.

If you're going above and beyond to help someone because you want their praise, their attention, or inclusion into their group, that's fitting in and not belonging. And, you're potentially robbing them of the benefit of self-discovery (i.e., working through their own sh*t).

If you're helping someone because you think they need to be *fixed*, that's judgement and will certainly feel out of alignment. Check-in with yourself on why this judgement is present.

So, what do boundaries look and sound like? Here are some examples of events that will show up in your life.

When people keep asking you to participate beyond your bandwidth, choose to be uncomfortable in the moment, by saying, "No," rather than live with the bitterness of saying, "Yes," long after this episode passes by.

When you dread conversations with friends and family, ask yourself why? If you find yourself constantly engaging in these conversations from a place of fear, resentment, or *shoulding* (Life Lesson #12), consider making a different choice. Consider taking a break from those interactions or changing how you participate. You're entitled to control over your time.

Keep promises to yourself. Make a plan and stick to it, even when others seek to co-opt your time for their own needs. Value your happiness over the illusion of making them happy.

One last thing: choosing yourself doesn't mean you're choosing against someone else. Healthy and clear boundaries are beneficial for everyone. And people that are setting their own boundaries will respect that you're creating and aware of yours.

Life Lesson Challenges
- How does people-pleasing show up in your life?
- What boundaries do you have in place right now? How do you protect or enforce those boundaries?
- How do you know when the fences around your boundaries are crumbling or faltering?
- What steps can you take to solidify boundaries around your energy and actions?
- Which values are you abandoning in order to make sure others are happy? How would setting clear boundaries change this?

LIFE LESSON 26

I Wish I Knew That the Universe Was Working *for* Me (Not against Me)

Synchronicity is rapidly becoming one of my favorite words and concepts. It describes that sense of things happening serendipitously. You wish you had five dollars in cash to buy a coffee, check your empty wallet and then check your jacket only to find a crumbled bill deep in one pocket. You attend a conference only to meet the exact person who can help you further your mission or idea. I used to write off these occurrences as mere happenstance, indicative of a hidden casual connection. I've realized, throughout this journey, that rather than digging into the occurrences to find a connection, and thereby satisfy my skeptical mind, I've learned to accept these events for what I believe they are: gifts from the Universe. Signs that I'm on the path I'm meant to walk.

❦ ❦ ❦ ❦ ❦ ❦

Dear Lisa,

You are a smart cookie, so you may be picking up that many of the lessons I'm sharing with you can often be distilled down to *mindset*. And, not surprisingly, this lesson is all about mindset and perspective.

Things happen to you during your life. Some things are easily categorized as *good* or *beneficial*; things like, winning the lottery, getting a raise, meeting your life partner.

Other occurrences are, at first glance, less beneficial. Things like abuse, trauma, arrests, serious illness, bankruptcy, or divorce.

I invite you to shift your perspective about *all* things that happen in your life: they are simply occurrences. Stuff happens. No judgement, good or bad. Just events.

Now, once you wrap your head around that, I'm gonna ratchet up the self-development discomfort index.

I'm gonna invite you to believe that all the events are happening *for* you. All of these situations are there FOR you.

The illness, the raise, the relationships, and the grief. All there FOR you to learn from, to swim in, to absorb and grow from.

It doesn't mean that you won't have emotional reactions to these events; that's normal and healthy.

Identify those emotions and own them. Don't let them own you, controlling your actions. You don't have to be at the effect of your emotions. You are in charge here.

My challenge to you is to believe that the Universe is working for you in the present, not just retrospectively. I know you can look back on your twenty years of life and recognize synchronistic patterns. Can you see them now, today, right this minute? Can you see how something unexpected or challenging that happened earlier today might be working in your favor?

Life Lesson Challenges
- Looking back at your life history, how has each major milestone served you, no matter how difficult it may have been in the moment?
- How would it feel to have this realization in the moment? What would need to change in your life and mindset for this to be true?
- What would change in your life if you welcomed each milestone as an opportunity to deepen your self-awareness and consciousness?

LIFE LESSON 27

I Wish I Knew How to Play and Rest without Guilt

'll be the first to admit that I'm a work-in-progress on playing and resting without guilt. The playing part comes easier for me, because I have a large number of hobbies to call on for some fun. Rest, on the other hand, continues to be a battleground. During this journey of self-discovery, I've cultivated the ability to listen to my body. It's easier to tell when I'm physical and mentally tired, versus when I'm trying to avoid something. I've learned to sit with that discomfort for a few minutes, digging into what's behind those feelings. If the answer keeps pointing towards fatigue, I'll coach myself through taking a twenty-minute nap. That may not seem like a huge accomplishment, but it is for me. If I'm avoiding a task and the tiredness is more of a decoy, I'll spend a few minutes doing some internal detective work to understand what's happening. That self-discussion may still end in a nap, but I do my best to uncover reasons for avoidance as they typically reoccur in other forms (think: existential Whack-A-Mole). There's no hard and fast formula, other than to making space for lightness and rejuvenation in my life. And, who wouldn't want that?

♦ ♦ ♦ ♦ ♦ ♦

Dear Lisa,

I invite you (strongly) to incorporate rest and play into your days.

Take a nap. Go for a leisurely walk without a destination in mind.

Your skin is starting to crawl and you're probably very tempted to turn the page, am I right? Time without purpose? Sounds like your own personal nightmare.

If I know you (and I *do*), you don't go for a run without measuring the miles or your pace. You don't take a class just for fun; you take it and push yourself to get an A. Everything is scored, tracked, or measured. Years down the road, you'll actually be able to monitor the number of steps you take each day, the time you spend asleep and your heart rate using only your wristwatch (note: more stock tips are warranted here).

I know the concept of *free time* is hard to grasp. You have shame tapes that play loudly in your head whenever you contemplate play. *I'm lazy, I'm selfish, I'm a freeloader, I'm irresponsible*. I get that. You've seen this modeled in your life. Your ability to be uber-productive is a source of pride. You enjoy being thought of as a workaholic.

I'm not saying this is going to be easy. I'm saying this is incredibly important to your long-term wellbeing. I am not sharing this advice to torment you; there are good reasons to incorporate play into your life.

Reason #1: It's inversely correlated with addiction, depression, and anxiety.[5]

Reason #2: Laughter and joy contribute to lower blood pressure, increased satisfaction, and overall life enjoyment.[6]

Reason #3: You only have one life. So, laugh a little.[7]

So, what exactly does *play* look like? I'm gonna help you out – since I know this is a stretch for you –and list some examples of unstructured fun:

- Watching a favorite movie with popcorn and candy (yes, candy),
- Going for a hike,
- Sex (I *realize* there's an inherent biological purpose here; you get the...point),
- Making snowmen and snow angels,
- Watching waves crash on the beach,
- Reading a non-school book and watching the sunset,
- Listening to live music at a local café,
- Visiting an art museum.

Here are some examples that would not qualify as *play* in your world:

- Competitive team sports (emphasis on competitive),
- Board games (unless you can detach from the outcome... which is unlikely),
- Amusement parks (just, no),
- Exercise with a goal in mind (have to run X miles, at Y pace, etc.).

---

5   Gray, P. 2011. *American Journal of Play*, 3(4): 443-463. *Link*
6   National Institute for Play, *http://www.nifplay.org/opportunities/person-al-health/*.
7   God/Source/Universe, infinity.

Like the topics we've covered in other chapters, play is most powerful as a practice, preferable a daily practice. I know you're busy with school (and you love school). I know that a shame tape around laziness and irresponsibility pops up every time you chose to do something other than school, work, or running.

Start with once a week and build up from there. Give it a try and notice how it changes your life.

And then, there's rest. Let's just pause for a moment so I can say (with love and empathy), you are *exhausted* right now. I know you, and you're reading this with dark circles under your eyes, hands shaking from crushing caffeine to keep you from sleeping, and your head heavy and fuzzy with fatigue.

I wish I knew when I was your age how amazing it feels to have a full night's sleep. A whole eight hours of rejuvenating, restorative sleep. The delicious feeling of settling into a comfy chair or bed for a post-lunch nap.

Confront the shame tapes keeping you super busy and structured all the time. Ask yourself, why you feel the need to over-schedule and over-commit? What are you really telling yourself? What would you have to believe about yourself and the world to build more downtime into your days?

You owe it to yourself.

Life Lesson Challenges
- What does *play* mean for you? What about rest?
- What does *play* mean for the people you share your life with (spouse, significant other, friends, family)?
- How much time are you devoting to play/unstructured free time each week? How much would you like to devote to *play?*
- How much sleep do you typically get each night? How do you ensure you get enough rest?
- What is getting less than optimal rest costing you?

LIFE LESSON 28

I Wish I Knew How Creative
I Really Am

In this modern day, creativity may take a back seat to the dozens of other things on our *long* to-do lists. It's often viewed as an indulgence, something to tackle when the *real* work of the day is done. Back when I first started experimenting with oil painting, I was mortified to show anyone what I'd created. It seemed to simplistic and childish. *What was the point of painting if I wasn't going to be a Picasso or a Stubbs?* That old shame tape around worthiness kept rearing its head. After working through these limiting beliefs, creativity has become the marriage of self-expression and play. I completely lose track of time when I'm writing, creating graphics, painting, or baking. Common types of creativity include painting, playing music, dancing, writing, knitting, and sketching. There are dozens more ways to explore your creativity. I have a feeling that if you start dabbling in these pursuits, you'll realize you're much more artistic and creative than you ever thought possible. And, you may just uncover a true passion. Even if you never show anyone what you create, the act of bringing something into existence – creating something from nothing – *is* the reward.

❦ ❦ ❦ ❦ ❦ ❦

Dear Lisa,

I know you've always liked to dabble with creative pursuits. The jewelry making class in high school. The numerous painting sets you've bought over the years: bought but never really used. You watched your mom and sister create incredible art with fabrics, yarn, and paint.

Persevere. Try things, even if it's only the one time. Use all those book smarts and create a story. Write a book (that's ironic). Paint a picture for your parents (they'll love it, trust me). Start scrapbooking (two words: glitter glue).

This may seem like I'm *shoulding* all over you, forcing my beliefs onto you and your life. Think of it as a strong invitation. Why? Because I know now what it's cost you over the years to bury that part of your essence.

Unused creativity stays bottled up inside and poisons our psyches, just as surely as too much junk food poisons our bodies. The longer you go without flexing those creativity muscles, the more difficult it will be become to create anything new. You will feel stuck in a rut. Repeating, regurgitating content, recycling thoughts and patterns.

There's only one way out of that rut. You need to get busy creating. Paint. Draw. Knit. String beaded necklaces. Sing. Dance. Play music. You don't have to try and commoditize these things. Just do them and experience the pure joy of creation.

Speaking of creativity, you are a gifted cook and baker. Not only are these creative pursuits; they also produce (usually) delicious results. Why not carve out one night a week for experimenting in the kitchen? Tweak a recipe, add your spin on a classic. And pay attention to how you feel when you're creating. What emotions arise? How does your body feel? What thoughts run through your head?

Remember the p-word from a few lessons back? *Practice*.

Find something, anything that taps into your self-expression. Get creative being creative (sorry, couldn't help myself).

It'll pay dividends far beyond the canvas, cake or crocheted blanket.

It'll feed your soul and crack open possibilities in all areas of life.

Life Lesson Challenges
- How often do you feel *stuck in a rut,* recycling the same thoughts, feelings, and actions?
- How does creativity show up in your life? When can you remember feeling creative in the past?
- What is (are) your favorite ways to explore your creativity? If nothing comes to mind, what creative pursuits would you like to try?
- What stops you from sticking to your creative time? What gets in the way?

LIFE LESSON 29

I Wish I Knew More About
My Emotions

like to think that I have a pretty expansive vocabulary. However, before I started on this journey, I was hard-pressed to name more than a handful of emotions, let alone recognize how they *felt* in my body or emerged in my *behavior*. I couldn't always directly link my self-narrative to my feelings. As I continue to work on self-awareness, I'm astounded by how powerful it is to 1) recognize dozens of emotions, 2) name my specific emotions and feelings in the moment, and 3) know what it feels like to consciously control my emotional response. My invitation to you: can you discern the difference between something like anger and frustration in your thoughts, feelings, and actions? What would change in your life if you had that razor-sharp awareness?

🌵 🌵 🌵 🌵 🌵 🌵

Dear Lisa,

Moving through the world – especially the decades you have in front of you – will be greatly improved by elevating your emotional intelligence. This is where your book smarts, and love of all things studying, is going to come in handy.

Emotional intelligence is defined by Webster's dictionary as, "the capacity to be aware of, control, and express one's emotions, and to handle interpersonal relationships judiciously and empathetically."

Let's start with the small stuff.

How are you feeling? Right now.

How many emotions can you name? Right now. Go.

If you haven't been able to list at least twenty emotions, you've got work to do.

Future research will consider twenty-seven as the minimum number of emotions we need to understand and recognize in order to function optimally.[8]

You can do this. You love school, right?

Start with the big ten:

- Joy,
- Excitement,
- Surprise,
- Sadness,
- Anger,
- Disgust,
- Contempt,
- Fear,
- Shame,
- Guilt.

---

8   A.S. Cowen and D. Keltner. 2017. *Proceedings of the National Academy of Sciences*, E7900-7909.

Try to figure out how you *feel* when you're experiencing these emotions. What sensations are present in your body? Role play in your mirror. Act angry, act surprised. How does your face change when shifting through those emotions? Really feel into it. Now, look back at your list. What other emotions can you add?

If you're feeling stuck, call upon a dictionary or thesaurus to populate your emotions list. Try to discern what it would feel like to experience all those emotions.

Why is this important? The quicker and easier you can recognize *exactly* what you're feeling, the more power you have to stay or shift out of that space. For example, cultivating this self-awareness will enable you to consciously choose whether to stay angry while driving or shift to a sense of awareness. Or stay angry. It revolves around choosing to experience the emotions that serve you and your highest purpose. You won't feel beholden to feeling whatever emotions arise. By naming and recognizing the specific emotions, you can decide how you'd like to proceed. You'll gain the power to choose how you want to feel.

And the power of choice, as we know, is the ultimate superpower.

Life Lesson Challenges
- Which emotions can you name?
- Which emotions can you recognize in yourself? How does this serve you?
- Which emotions can you recognize in others? How does this impact your life?
- How successful are you in shifting into or out of specific emotional states? What does this success depend on?
- What would change in your life if you were more adept at recognizing and shifting emotional states?
- What does feeling at the effect of your emotions cost you? Why?

LIFE LESSON 30

I Wish I Knew That Learning Happens all the Time, Not Just During School

This may seem obvious to you (and maybe it is); I've struggled in the past with over-identifying with my credentials. Education and learning only really had value in my mind in if were attached to a degree or certificate. You may remember that this was directly related to my shame tape around *not being smart enough*. What I know now, is that some of the most valuable and long-lasting education experiences took place outside the classroom. There are a lot of phrases to describe this concept: street smarts, *real world* intelligence, savvy. I am where I am today because I gained the street smarts necessary to fully leverage my formal education. There is synergy there; a magic brew. And, if I'm being honest, my intuition is always my greatest teacher.

Dear Lisa,

This lesson is right in your wheelhouse. Sort of.

You are a lifelong student, that much is clear. (And there's more school in your future!)

I know you love that feeling of cracking open a fresh spiral notebook on the first day of class. The paper is all creamy white with blue stripes; the pink line cascading down the page. It's just waitin' for some *knowledge*.

The thing is…not everything you will need to thrive on your journey can be found in a textbook.

The lessons you will learn from life will add to your knowledge base in a way that classroom education cannot.

You'll learn more about yourself, the way the world works, the armor people (and you!) wear, the deep truths behind someone's lies, the depths of another's soul. You'll learn how extraordinarily strong and courageous you are, how much you have to offer the world. You'll learn to recognize a whole spectrum of human emotions. You'll learn to cultivate trust and vulnerability.

How will you learn these things?
- Connecting with people,
- Having the courage to cultivate close relationships,
- Recognizing when relationships have run their course,
- Burying your loved ones,
- Traveling around the world,
- Cultivating self-compassion,
- Setting big goals and achieving them,

- Working hard and accepting opportunities when they're offered,
- Moving to new cities.

The danger in keeping your nose firmly between the textbook pages, is that you're missing out on experiences that make you three-dimensional. What do I mean by that? If you only focus on that formal education, you are only playing one note, you only have one song in your repertoire. Now, it's undoubtedly a beautiful song. How would it feel to play a symphony, to hear all those instruments, harmonies, and chords combined together?

Enrich your life, expand your world-view, feed your neurons. Raise your hand when people ask for volunteers. Be all in. Be the symphony.

Life Lesson Challenges
- Looking back, what lessons are most memorable from your school days?
- What life lessons outside of school have been the most impactful?
- How do you cultivate learning outside of the classroom?
- Where, in your life, do you resist taking chances or making change? Why? What lies beneath that resistance?

LIFE LESSON 31

I Wish I Knew (and Believed) That It's Always Darkest Before the Dawn

There is a reason that clichés become clichés: they hold a nugget of truth. I love this lesson because I can look back on my life and see the moments when I gave in, even though I was just days or hours away from the *breakthrough* I was desperately hoping for; I gave into the darkness. Of course, you'll say, hindsight is always 20-20 (another accurate cliché!). True. I would argue that I can pinpoint the moment when I told myself that the sun will never rise. I knew when I gave in on certain dreams or goals because I couldn't see how it would get better. Or, I couldn't see how I could accomplish it. When I did find the strength to keep going, I was often surprised by how much I was capable of giving or doing. Almost like time and self-doubt led me to under-estimate my reserves of grit and ability. Food for thought.

❦ ❦ ❦ ❦ ❦ ❦

Dear Lisa,

With everything you'll tackle in your life, no one would dare call you a quitter. I know you take a lot of pride in finishing what you start. *I don't give up*, you'll tell people. It's just not part of our DNA.

Some call this ability *perseverance* or *grit*. Others call it stubbornness or pig-headedness, usually depending on whether or not your grittiness works in their favor!

You'll hear this cliché over and over: it's always darkest before the dawn.

It's easy and tempting to scoff at these clichés! Until you realize that they ring true.

You'll encounter many situations over your life that call upon your grit. You'll often call upon those emotional and mental reserves to meet those life milestones. Things like competing in high school sports, finishing college, completing graduate school, finishing IRONMAN races. In these earlier decades of your life, grit seems easy to come by.

As you get older, perseverance will be more challenging to tap into on a regular basis. You'll still set ambitious goals for yourself. You'll still keep your standards high. But, instead of immediately rising to the occasion, a new instinct will arise: *rationalization*.

You'll start to find reasons to back away from your goals and dreams when the going gets tough. When you're challenged to grow or adapt, you'll feel that urge to deflect and avoid descend over your life.

Remember that dream you've had since you were little, your dream to start a bakery? You do it! You start a home-based bakery business, wading through paperwork, forms, and logistical hurdles to make that dream come true. You called upon your grit and self-belief. And, for several months, the bakery business will boom! You'll sell out every day, you'll get asked to make desserts for a local restaurant. Everything you wanted will be placed in front of you. You rent a commercial kitchen and start cranking out pastries and pies into the wee hours of the morning. And, you'll start to panic a little. The bills will start mounting up. You'll start to second guess the decision to follow this dream in the first place. You'll hang in there for three months until you, literally, can't afford to anymore. It'll be a dark time; very dark and lonely.

So, you'll make the heart-wrenching decision to walk away from the bakery. You'll close down the commercial kitchen, send out notices to your customers, and pack all the equipment away in your garage. It'll break your heart to walk away. It'll seem impossible that you'd recover, that you will find something that will capture your imagination the same way.

The truth is, you did follow your dream. Maybe it wasn't the right time. Maybe, if you had figured out a way to expand the bakery, it would've ceased to fulfill you. Maybe, you would have made the bakery business your life's mission.

The point is, no matter how dark those times feel, the dawn will always come. Not necessarily as we expect or want it to (i.e., a miracle loan handed to you, to keep the bakery running), but the sun will always rise and relight your passion for life.

In this case, the *dawn* after your bakery business closed was realizing that you don't have to commoditize your hobbies for them to be valid, noble pursuits.

Another great example of how this will show up for you is something we talked about way back in Life Lesson #2, the reality that breaking down means breaking through. You will nearly get lost in the darkness before you embark on this self-development journey. But the dawn most certainly came.

So, my invitation for you, is to believe that you will survive the darkest moments, that the dawn will bring new dreams and new possibilities. It always does. Always.

Life Lesson Challenges
- How does grit and perseverance show up in your life?
- Looking back, is there a goal or a dream you wish you'd kept pursuing? What lessons can you take from that experience?
- Can you pinpoint the reason you changed your mind toward a goal or dream? What insights can you gain? If you knew then what you know now, what would you do differently?

LIFE LESSON 32

I Wish I Knew How to Discern
Attraction from Love

Let me be clear, dear reader, there is nothing *wrong* with attraction. We are biologically hard-wired to be attracted to other humans. We are literally *designed* to be attracted to each other. We send out and receive chemical signals that trigger all sorts of reactions in our physical and emotional bodies. You know what I'm talking about. That's how our species evolved and...*ahem*...propagated. That patterning probably isn't gonna disappear anytime soon. Not having this discernment certainly caused no small amount of confusion in my life. It's a lesson I would've liked to have known way back when.

Dear Lisa,

Love. Attraction. How many lives have been lost (and created) over the centuries because of these?

You don't have to look far back in our cultural past to understand how powerful the grip of attraction can be. Remember your high school history?

Love, as I'm defining it, is a deep, spiritual connection paired with mutual respect and trust. Love with may include a romantic or sexual component but doesn't require it. Love and attraction can (and does) co-exist. This lesson focuses on not confusing attraction with deep connection

So, what's the story, here? Why the need to separate attraction and love? Aren't they two sides of the same coin? Yes. And no.

Yes, because the first blush of attraction *can* lead to the richer, deeper experience of mutual love.

No, because you will experience that intense rush of attraction and that is often where the story ends (or must end). Which is fine. Unless, you force the issue and try to reframe that attraction as love, as long-term intimacy without a foundation of mutual respect, trust, or reciprocity. In other words, unrequited love. This is only setting yourself up for failure and heartbreak. Not because you're not lovable; rather because love requires the involvement of both parties. Attraction can and often is a one-way street.

You will encounter situations where you feel a strong attraction to a specific person. I invite you to accept that feeling of attraction and then consciously decide what (if anything) to do about it.

I invite you to avoid acting on attraction from a place of lack or a desire to *prove* to yourself that you're loveable. Again, consider this a slippery slope towards dissatisfaction and self-loathing.

Just because you feel the attraction doesn't mean that love is a guaranteed outcome. It can just be attraction. You can love the thrill of those biochemical messengers racing through your body. The danger you face is mis-reading those messages as directives. *You must love this person, why else would you be attracted to them? Quick! Turn your life upside down to connect with them and build a life together*!

If you feel attracted to someone and act on it, enjoy! I'm not arguing for self-judgment; I'm arguing for discernment of intent.

Check in with your self-narrative and the messages your body is sending you. Figure out what your intention is behind pursuing a relationship with someone.

Life Lesson Challenges
- How do you discern the difference between love and attraction in your romantic relationships?
- When, if at all, have you experienced unrequited love? What did this cost you?
- What advice would you give yourself about the difference between attraction and love?

LIFE LESSON 33

I Wish I Knew How to Avoid
Co-Dependency

Similar to the love vs. attraction lesson (*Life Lesson #32*), this is all about being aware and clear about what relationships are and are not, and your intention behind cultivating the relationship. One of my core values is service. Helping others, putting their needs above mine is a default setting for me. This is a wonderful attribute *until* I tip over into co-dependency, victim-thinking, and enmeshment. When I neglect my boundaries, when I succumb to the shame tapes in my mind, I give away my power and start relying on other people for my happiness and succor. It's a slippery slope to self-blame and some pretty dark times.

Dear Lisa,

Let's start with some definitions, courtesy of Webster's dictionary, just so you and I are on the same page.

A *relationship* is, "the way in which two or more concepts, objects, or people are connected, or the state of being connected." This includes romantic and platonic relationships.

Co-dependency is, "excessive emotional or psychological reliance on a partner or person."

The key word here is *reliance*.

You rely on the other person to determine everything. Your happiness. Your anger. Your fear. Your life choices. Your diet.

Believe it or not, co-dependency will be a part of your life for a few years. You'll get involved in a long-term relationship that does not bring out the best in you. What I know now, is that you entered that relationship from a place of lack. If I don't say, "Yes," to this person, I may never get asked again. Totally understandable that you would feel that way, especially since this was your first serious relationship. Wanting to be a *good* girlfriend, you start subsuming your personality to fit in with your new partner.

You can't make a decision or a choice unless the other person signs off on it. You wait to eat a meal until they sit down, not because you're being polite or want to share a meal, but because you don't feel capable of doing anything on your own.

You are unable to identify where your needs start and end. Every decision requires input.

At first, this feels comfortable, almost companionable. You're sharing your life with someone, right? You're sharing decisions, you value their opinion.

Sure, I totally get that. It's a slippery slope, though.

And, once you're in that place where the needs and self-identity are completely enmeshed with someone else, you've lost something incredibly important: *yourself*.

My challenge to you: recognize the signs that you may be in a co-dependent relationship.

When you can't make a decision without someone else weighing in—stop. Hang up the phone. Walk away. Get help. Talk to a therapist or a coach.

Ask yourself why you're thinking, feeling and acting this way. Be relentless when exploring these self-narratives, keep asking *why* until you arrive at an answer.

Life Lesson Challenges
- If your default response is to put others' needs ahead of your own, how can you tell when you cross over into co-dependency?
- Have you ever found yourself in a relationship that bore the hallmarks of co-dependency, that sense of excessive reliance on your partner?
- Have you been involved in a relationship when someone was excessively reliant on you? How did that impact your experience in that relationship?
- If you've walked away from a co-dependent relationship, how did you make that choice? What lessons did you learn from that experience?

LIFE LESSON 34

I Wish I Knew How to Consistently Tap into My 'Why'

I am blessed with an ability to participate and enjoy a wide variety of activities. From triathlons to baking, to reading, art, and science, my hobbies and passions run the gamut. I struggle sometimes with not being able to pinpoint exactly what my purpose is – am I someone who just likes variety? Am I fickle and flighty? Am I indecisive? As I continued on my journey, I've realized – with support from a brilliant coach - that at the center of all of these activities is my core purpose: self-expression. Once I had that realization, I stopped judging myself so harshly. All of the activities that brought me joy and fulfillment fit into the *why* of self-expression. All roads lead to Rome, in other words. This realization lifted that heavy cloud of self-judgment and searching, allowing me to really lean fully into the joy, and keep that *why* of self-expression firmly in my sights.

✹ ✹ ✹ ✹ ✹ ✹

Dear Lisa,

Passion and purpose are two of the most important things to cultivate in life. For you, one typically connects with the other. A passion leads to a purpose and vice versa.

I know that you have no shortage of ideas and hobbies. The concept of your *why* goes deeper than that.

Passion is something that wakes you up in the middle of the night. The drive to create, to change, to move mountains, to *climb* mountains. The *compulsion* to pursue something is the juicy center of life.

There'll be a lot of days and weeks that you'll feel like you're punching your timecard. There'll be a sense of monotony and repetition, which can be very mind-numbing. I get it.

My challenge to you: make the most of those monotonous times. Even if that means reigniting your passion for your current job. Figure *why* you want to be there. The *why* is the magic key.

Fly on auto-pilot if you have to and take time to dream. Stoke that fire in your belly while you are pumping out those widgets and slide presentations.

Speaking of dreaming and searching for your life purpose, here are some suggestions on how to narrow down what your *why* might be right now:

- What could you do for hours and not notice the passage of time?
- What do you find yourself day-dreaming about while working?
- If you had all the money and time in the world, what would you do?
- Who's life and work do you admire? Why?

That's the surefire way to figure out what that next passion (and purpose) will be.

Life Lesson Challenges
- What is your passion? Why? What do you want your purpose to be?
- How did you answer the questions above? What did you learn about yourself?
- What would change in your life, if you followed that passion and purpose?
- What would happen if you integrate that *why* into your current life and work?
- What gets in the way of following your passion and life purpose?

LIFE LESSON 35

I Wish I Knew That Gossip is Really Just Judgement in Disguise

This lesson dovetails with the earlier discussion around judgement (see Life Lesson #4). I felt it was worth re-visiting for two reasons. One, repetition of key concepts is never a bad thing. And, two, I remember this flavor of judgement consuming a lot of my corporate working hours. In other words, I used to judge my co-workers and colleagues, and engage in gossip about fellow workers. I'm not proud of that behavior. I can look back now and recognize how hurt and scared I was in those moments, how shame threatened to choke me and how good it felt to dispel those feelings by picking on other people. I may not have outwardly expressed these judgements, but I did plenty of gossiping in corners and behind people's backs. It sickens me to realize that I held such poison in my mind and heart for years. It's a wrong I wish I could remedy, person to person; while that may not be possible, I *can* apologize here for that disrespect. I'm sorry. I offer no excuses; only explanations. It was all my sh*t. It had nothing to do with you. That's what I've come to learn about gossip and it's a lesson I try to live every day.

* * * * * *

Dear Lisa,

I know. I see you shaking your head at this lesson's topic!

It can seem like the person who is constantly late to work and unprepared for meetings is not doing their best. My invitation to you: ask yourself if you *know* (not believe or want to believe) that this is true. *Then their best isn't good enough*, you say. I get it.

Let me tell you a story. Your first real job after grad school will bring you up to Boston (get those Celtics season tickets, you won't regret it!). The company will be great, you'll meet wonderful people.

This environment will also activate your dormant judgement gene. *As in, I'm better than the rest of you fat, lazy, imbecilic slobs.* Yep. It won't be pretty.

You'll get caught up in gossip and judging people. Your razor-sharp wit will make quick work of other people's frailties, slashing their soft emotional under-bellies for the amusement of other gossipers. You'll feel that warm glow of fitting in when others share in your judgement. The deeper your shame is around certain topics - the more you're hurting - the stronger the vitriol you spew.

That's just the way the world works, you'll tell yourself. You'll come up with a dozen rationalizations for your behavior: *It's a* shark tank, bite first or be bitten. I'm not the only one acting this way. Fear is an effective motivator.

One day, you'll be walking through the hallway of a big company, just about to emerge around the corner of a small kitchen area. It's a place everyone gathers between meetings and meals to chat or grab coffee. You'll hear your name mentioned. You'll hear a nasty comment. Then you'll hear snickering. As you turn the corner – face flushed, heart hammering in your chest, the fight/flight/freeze instinct kicking in – you'll see three close colleagues. And, you'll know (finally) what it feels like to have that poison splash back on you. They will glance at you coldly, daring you to respond. You will slink away, sickened that you have been perpetrating that same toxic emotional violence against others, all from a place of fear and unworthiness.

Judging, gossiping, and bullying is the easy path, the chicken sh*t path...and yes, that's a judgement!

The good news is, you can change this pattern. It's never too late to try.

Check your worse impulses (we all have them!). When you feel yourself sliding down this slope, press pause. Step away and connect with your self-narrative.

Are you really seeking to solve a problem or are you seeking to dispel your own discomfort? What is your intention behind this impulse?

Be vigilant around desires to belittle or judge; use these as indicators that all is not right with *you*.

Life Lesson Challenges

Stop what you're doing. And look up from this page. Look around.

- What is underneath a desire to judge someone else against the standard you've set for them? Why? Where did that impulse come from?

- How true is it that you know with 100% certainty that they aren't doing their best?
- How would it feel to release that judgement? What would shift for you?

LIFE LESSON 36

I Wish I Knew That Rehearsing Loss Doesn't Mean Avoiding Grief

For years, I never really understood what was happening to me during the moments I describe in the lesson below. I truly thought I was suffering from post-traumatic stress disorder (PTSD). After doing some research (and speaking with a therapist), I now believe that I was experiencing a PTSD-like reaction, not from the experience of past violent trauma but from my inability to ease fully into joy for fear of loss. In other words, I was foreboding joy. I learned about this phenomenon and the antidote from reading Brene Brown's work. This knowledge and awareness has dramatically changed my life, for which I am forever grateful. For more information on foreboding joy, its relationship to vulnerability and the power of gratitude, check out the works from Brene Brown listed in the *Additional Resources* section at the back of the book.

🌵 🌵 🌵 🌵 🌵 🌵

Dear Lisa,

As part of your need to control outcomes, you'll often find yourself rehearsing disappointment, loss, or pain.

For example, you may find yourself thinking and visualizing how you'd react if a family member passes away. You may try to rehearse what you'd say, how you'd say it, how you'd feel and how others will react to you.

You'll think, *Check, all done. Loss won't get the jump on me.*

You'll say to yourself, *After all, I am nothing if not a gifted learner. So, I should be able to learn how to avoid grief, right?*

Not so much. You will learn, firsthand, that rehearsals do not allow you to opt out of grief or pain, when life's eventualities occur. Instead, they just rob you of joy in the here and now. (See Life Lesson #21 around Numbing). Remember, you can't select numb: taking down the grief means taking down the joy.

Years from now, you will be sitting on the couch in your front room. Both of your dogs will be sleeping peacefully around you. Your partner will be studying at his desk, head phones on and deep in concentration. The early morning light will be streaming in through the double windows. Bliss. Peace. Togetherness. One of life's simple, pure moments of joy. You'll feel a deep gratitude and contentment bubble up in your chest. And then...*bam*!

In your mind's eye, you see a huge truck crash through the front windows, slam into the room at full speed, crushing your partner, killing your dogs. Broken glass, carnage, smoking engine, gas fumes. Your house looks like the aftermath of an action movie crash scene. And you sit there on the couch paralyzed with fear, wide-eyed, dripping with sweat and shaking with fear. Horrible, right?

This will happen over and over again; so much so, that you'll start to question: *Why do you have to play these horrific scenes out? What is going on?*

What you didn't know and what you'll eventually learn, is that this is very normal and happens when people lose their ability to feel joy. Basically, it's like asking for ice cream, getting the ice cream and then being too afraid of the ice cream being taken away that you sit there paralyzed. It's irrational because it's based in fear.

It's tempting for you to just quash this instinct, to ignore it, to shove it away. If we've learned anything on this journey together, you know that ignoring this type of reaction also makes it worse.

Thanks to ground-breaking research, you learn about the antidote to these incredibly disruptive experiences:

- Focus on the present moment and look around at the room.
- Take a few deep breaths, letting the air flow slowly in and out of your body.
- Find something to be grateful for in that exact moment.
- Be specific and focus on that feeling of gratitude.
- Tell yourself you're grateful for this moment, your family, the sun, the grass, the sky, anything and everything you can see.

This brings you into the present moment, stopping that catastrophe tape from playing.

Not only will this practice bring you fully into the present, it will elevate your emotions and reset the physical sensations. The fear and anxiety will slowly be replaced by a sense of calm, allowing you to ride out the storm.

Life Lesson Challenges
- Do you find yourself rehearsing tragedy or grief? If so, how and when does this show up?
- How would it feel to redirect your energy to the present using gratitude to snap out of that mindset?
- What would change for you?

LIFE LESSON 37

I Wish I Knew That Jealousy Works the Opposite Way You Want It To

would not consider myself especially fluent in the language of romantic relationships. Perhaps you've already picked up on that. There have certainly been times when my self-esteem challenges emerged as intense jealousy. In those moments, I was not equipped to dissect why I was battling with possessiveness and gremlin messages around not being loveable. I now understand the patterns and sensations that indicate my jealousy self-narrative has started up. What I didn't appreciate back then was that jealousy weakens relationships *not* strengthens them. I'm not proud of how I behaved in those jealous moments – typically fueled by excessive amounts of alcohol – I can only apologize and share that I know now I was hurting and desperate for proof of worthiness. Which are normal, human conditions. Of all the lessons I've learned over the years, really putting this awareness of jealousy's inherent paradox into practice, has brought me (and probably my partner) comfort and peace.

🌵 🌵 🌵 🌵 🌵 🌵

Dear Lisa,

There will be moments when jealousy will take over your life. You will be in a committed and loving relationship, enjoying some social event, and then - *Boom!* – the green mist descends.

Example: you are out at a local bar with your guy, throwing back the drinks, laughing it up and your eye will notice a particularly attractive woman on the other side of the room. In your drunken haze, you think you'll see your guy gaze longingly at her, ignoring you completely.

Now, in reality, he may indeed be checking her out. It's part of being human, after all. We check each other out. Did he gaze longingly at her and start contemplating how to ditch you for her? That is the exact message your jealousy gremlin is screaming at you, helped along by the tequila shots.

Jealousy boils down to you feeling less than or not enough. You will, in these moments, often hear the shame tapes of *not sexy enough, not beautiful enough, not skinny enough, not exciting enough*. Just know that it is normal to feel that way. Your instinct at this point in your journey, is to attack yourself, then transform all that shame into blame and shove it onto your partner. You blame him for not loving you enough, for deserting you, for betraying you. You work yourself into a jealous rage, yell, break things, and make choices are not consistent with your values.

The reality is...it has *nothing* to do with him. Jealousy is another way of saying that you are wrestling with your own demons...er, gremlins.

Knowing what I know now, I would invite you to look that green-eyed monster in the eye and confront those gremlins. If that means you need to leave a social situation when the surge envelops you and find a quiet place to think, do it. Ask yourself what's really underneath your jealousy. What is the narrative running through your mind? What story are you telling yourself about what's happening?

Let's say you are telling yourself that your partner doesn't love you anymore because he's making polite conversation with another woman.

Fact check yourself. How true is it that you know for a fact this narrative is true? The truth is, you don't know that. You are driving yourself crazy trying to explain away a perfectly normal situation by grabbing onto a self-destructive narrative. This also very much falls under calling yourself on your bullsh*t (Life Lesson #15).

So, what's a woman to do?

Once you can fact check those shame narratives, ask yourself how the best version of yourself would show up. Would she laugh it off? Would she walk over, introduce herself, and join the conversation? Would she look over, catch her guy's eye and wink playfully? Or, maybe she needs a few minutes of deep breathing and a walk to clear her head.

One other suggestion— stop drinking so much. Cut that sh*t out. Stop going for long runs before a planned night out and then skipping dinner so you feel skinnier (see Life Lesson 7 on *Loving Yourself*). Stop feeding your gremlins with tequila.

The only thing stopping you from showing up *sans* jealousy is *you*.

Life Lesson Challenges

- How does jealousy show up in your life? What impact does it have?
- Where does this jealousy come from? What are your self-narratives during flashes of jealousy?
- What would it look and feel like to show up without jealousy? What would need to change to make that a reality?

LIFE LESSON 38

I Wish I Knew How to Make Money My Friend Not My Enemy

Money can be an emotionally charged subject. It certainly was for me not that long ago. The mere mention of a bill, or my checking account, or my student loans would twist my stomach into knots and make my eyes well up. Ugh, I felt powerless to make or control money. And, it's not just because I'm not inherently a numbers-person. I certainly have the necessary arithmetic skills to work with money. I just had a hard time de-criminalizing it. Money was the root of all evil. If I wanted to make (more of) it, I was greedy. If I wanted to save it, I was a skin-flint. If I wanted to spend it, I was irresponsible. That mindset really kept me trapped in a fiscal no-win situation for years; and made me miserable to boot. I'd love to tell you that there's one life hack or a trick to making this change. For me, it was a gradual, relentless erosion of all the myths I'd created around money. And I certainly didn't do that alone. I had an amazing finance whiz of a partner who patiently talked me off the proverbial ledge. I devoured books geared toward changing one's money mind. With this help, I revolutionized how I approach and view money. Check out the *Additional Resources* section for a list of suggested readings around this topic.

* * * * * *

Dear Lisa,

There will be many times in you're life when your bank account balance (or lack thereof) will make scarcity seem a logical state of affairs. I mean, numbers don't lie, right? When it says you have -$75 in your account, there's not much room for interpretation. You can forgive yourself for feeling less than flush in those moments.

However, even when you're earning a generous salary, you'll constantly fight the feeling that there's never going to be *enough* money or that you'll never have the right amount of money at a given time. This will start in college when your student loan disbursement at the start of each semester will make you feel *flush* right up until you run out of money two weeks before classes end. At which point, it'll be more rock bottom, less Rockefeller.

You'll keep grasping and clawing at the promise of more money throughout grad school, learning how to live creatively below the poverty line.

Then, you'll land your first *real* job: real salary, real benefits, real 401K. You'll look at the offer letter and nearly pass out at the number of zeros behind your salary. Ignoring the fact that you were moving to one of the most expensive parts of the country (from one of the least expensive), you'll leverage that offer letter to buy an unnecessarily expensive car. It will be ostentatious and non-ecofriendly. And bright red. And, you'll love it. You'll rationalize why you need a SUV that large for the move up north (it snows up there, right? Four-wheel drive. Check).

This is the start of what I'll call your *whiplash* relationship with money. Save and spend, both in equally large measures, but never in a logical way. You'll pinch pennies at the grocery store and buy a pair of $400 boots (super cute, sure, but still).

You'll live paycheck to paycheck for the better part of 20 years. Even though you'll make good money – some years even *great* money – you will treat money like the scum at the bottom of the garbage can. You can see it's there but the thought of cleaning it out is *way* too disturbing. Better to leave it alone all together.

You buy a house you don't really want in a place that quadruples your daily commute so that your dog could have a backyard. Admirable, sure, but the commute will drive you crazy (pun intended) and you'll end up renting an apartment closer to work. So now you have two housing payments. I don't need to delve into on differential equations here to convince you that this is a recipe for financial disaster.

So, you'll treat that house and its mortgage like garbage can gunk. If you don't look too closely at it, maybe it'll disappear. You'll spend ten months doing this dance, each month red-lining your income, the unoccupied house a ticking time bomb.

On a bitterly cold day in January, after a week of record low temps, you'll pull into the driveway of that forgotten house and see a torrent of water and ice streaming down the outside of a fractured front room window. Not a good sign.

That frozen pipe will dictate your credit and financing history for the next decade. It's the harbinger of a disastrous attempt at a short sale, a foreclosure, and a precipitous credit plunge.

Years of turning a blind eye to your finances will haunt you. It'll take years to rebuild your credit, pay down the debt, and erase the foreclosure.

Only when you start to see money as part of your life *energy* will the situation start to shift. It'll suck at first. It'll feel like it's never going to get better. There is no light, only darkness. I get it. I know.

The turning point is changing your mindset. Money is *not* the enemy. Money, or lack thereof, doesn't hold *you* back. Money can always be obtained. You can always tap into that well, if you need it.

Don't believe me?

Go to your closet right now. Got any clothes you could sell? Go to the garage. Got any bikes you can sell?

Walk down Main Street. Anyone looking for part-time help?

Money is not the barrier. Your *mindset* that you don't have to change your existence or daily routine to obtain money is a barrier. That money will somehow just land in your lap to erase all the self-destructive decisions you've made – that is the true barrier.

Start today. Start now.

Here's how:

- Live, breathe, sleep, and eat abundance mentality. Believe that you have enough, that you will always have enough.
- Force yourself to look at your bank account and credit card balances.
- Take control. Know when money is coming in and where it needs to go.

- Pay bills first.
- Pay debts first.
- Set aside a little fun money each week (note—I said a *little*).
- Ask for help when you need it. Ask for lower interest rates. Ask to skip a payment if you need to, don't just ignore it.
- Sell things you don't love or wear anymore.
- Impose a 90-day moratorium on shopping other than food and basic necessities.
- Get a part-time job over the holidays for extra cash.
- Save more than you spend (this is a DUH, right? So, why aren't you?).

I know this list may sound obvious but, trust me, it bears repeating.

The more you can embrace this new mindset, the more you can take control, the more you'll start to see money as a currency of transformation in your life, not a barrier to living. The quicker you can see money as energy – neither good nor bad – the quicker you'll be able to make peace with this essential part of our human experience.

As this lesson title suggests, treat money like a trusted, loved friend. Don't cling to your dollars and don't take them for granted. Cherish them, love them, cultivate that relationship and know how to create healthy boundaries around money.

There are few lessons in this book that will serve you more than this one. Do yourself a favor, learn it now and learn it well.

Life Lesson Challenges
- How would you describe your relationship with money?
- How could that relationship improve?

- If your money mindset is less than ideal, what is this costing you (in more than just money)?
- What would change in your life if you embraced the abundance mentality?
- What would stop you from living *abundantly*?

LIFE LESSON 39

I Wish I Knew How to Change Intentionally

Some people will look at my life journey and question whether or not I need a lesson in embracing change. I have, after all, lived in nearly every part of the country, moved more than four dozen times, quit my job and moved to a remote tropical island, and held a dozen different jobs during my adult life. It would seem, on the surface, that I'm good with change. Yes, I'm capable of change and transition. But why the compulsion to change? Is it fear-based? Am I escaping a difficult situation rather than facing it? Is my intuition guiding me to the next step in my journey? These aren't questions I asked myself until very recently. The pace of change in my life hasn't slowed down; I've just stepped off the rollercoaster. I've learned to pivot when it will help me reach my goals more quickly, not because

I can't face the reality I've chosen. This lesson is really more about cultivating awareness of why I'm seeking change in my life, the intention behind the transition.

❈ ❈ ❈ ❈ ❈ ❈

Dear Lisa,

This lesson really has two components:
- Examine your decision to join or say, "Yes," to something/someone when you really don't want to (see Life Lesson #25 on *Boundaries*),
- Examine the compulsion to reverse your decision.

The first component is all about boundaries – which we know you struggle with – and as a people pleaser, you often find yourself over-committed and overwhelmed.

Learning to say, "No," in the first place, when you're asked to contribute or participate in something that you clearly don't have interest in or bandwidth for, saves you from the one-two punch of guilt and resentment.

As a kind, empathetic person you often shy away from changing plans because you don't want to disappoint someone, fearing that you'll be ostracized or disliked.

You'll avoid having that difficult conversation, leaning into that discomfort, telling someone that the plan you'd made no longer works for you. That's totally understandable and completely natural.

Having the courage to change your mind really means looking inward, reflecting on whether this impulse is fear-motivated or values-driven.

If the first, consider having the courage to stick to your plan as a learning experience. If that latter, have the courage to speak up and let people know you've changed your mind.

This will show up in your life in small and big ways. You'll make plans to see movies, or have lunch, then want to cancel. You'll declare a major and then want to change. You'll go to graduate school and decide not to stay in academia. The decision to make these changes all require courage.

My advice: the bigger the impact of the decision on your life, the deeper you want to delve into the intentions behind the change. Not second guess or berate yourself, but an objective analysis and consideration.

Cancelling dinner plans? Take a minute or two to think about it.

Quitting your job and moving across country? Spend a few days thinking through and asking yourself enough questions, enough times, to get past the superficial *get-me-the-eff-out-of-here* escape feeling and down to your underlying motivations.

Remember: you are making decisions *for* you not against anyone else.

While these changes may trigger your *selfish* and *irresponsible* shame tapes, hang in there and stay curious. Be responsible for your feelings and your choices, not anyone else's.

Be brave and be clear.

You only have one life.

Don't spend it sticking to your guns when having the courage to change your mind is the best possible thing. You always have a choice.

Life Lesson Challenges
- Look back at the major changes or pivotal decisions in your life. Can you identify the intentions behind those changes? What takeaways do you have from that exercise?

- What changes are you resisting because you feel afraid to make different choices?
- How does it feel to know that you always have a choice?
- When do you most often feel that choices are hard to see?

LIFE LESSON 40

I Wish I Knew How to
Live Like My Dogs

Clearly, I'm not the first person to suggest that we learn to act more like dogs (or cats). I can, however, confidently say that I neglected to learn anything from my first dozen years as a dog owner. I saw them only as kid-substitutes rather than the unique, complex creatures that they really are. I am grateful to have had the privilege of learning those lessons with our two latest canine companions, Jordan and Kona. They are the yin and yang of the dog world. Jordan is a relaxed, chilled, lap jockey, content to snooze all day, and loves to hunt little lizards in the sun on our patio. But Kona is volcanic (hence the name), has frenetic energy, digs holes and chases squirrels for *hours*, hates being clean, does everything passionately (even sleeping). As I type this, Kona is jumping on me, wanting her dinner (she has a very precise schedule) while Jordan snores loudly nearby on her bed. Watching them romp and ramble around our yard fills with me such a profound sense of joy, love, and gratitude that I have trouble expressing it. I know they'll leave me one day not long from now. The thought brings unimaginable pain and sadness to me. But, they're not thinking about that. They just live their lives. So, I think I'll wrap this lesson up and go play outside with them one last time before the sun sets.

🌵 🌵 🌵 🌵 🌵 🌵

Dear Lisa,

I know you've always loved animals. From the time you could walk, you were surrounded by menageries: dogs, cats, rabbits, hamsters, horses.

As you grew up, the love deepened and you will spend your adult life in the presence of at least one dog, at all times.

There are so many lessons to learn from sharing your life with an animal.

First, *live for the moment.* Dogs – and most animals – live for each moment. They don't worry about what's going to happen tomorrow, they don't stew over what happened yesterday. They don't expend unnecessary energy worrying. They just *are*. Sounds nice, right?

Next, *don't play the shame game.* Dog's aren't ashamed of their bodies or looks. They don't wrestle with feeling lazy or unproductive. They are 100% sure that whatever they're doing is exactly what they should be doing at any given moment. Until they see a squirrel.

Next, *listen to your body*. Dogs may not see it this way, exactly, but they are instinctive and intuitive creatures. They rest when they're tired, seek shade when they're too warm, follow their instincts (and sometimes that squirrel right through the fence), seek quiet when they're hurt, and never say no to a treat.

Next, *find joy in the little things, in everything*. Your dogs will be just as happy chasing a leaf as tearing apart a cardboard box. They'll love the $5 toy as much (or more) than the $30 one (Yes, you'll spend *that* much on a dog toy. For real.). They are as content with simple affection as they are with long rounds of playing fetch or wrestling. *Every day is their best day.*

Finally, and perhaps most important, *love unconditionally and mirror back the love you receive*. Your animals know when they're loved and return that love wholeheartedly, without reservations. They are always happy to see you when you come home. They'll bring toys to you, snuggle with you on the couch, give you kisses when you cry, and celebrate with you.

Love deeply, knowing that there's always a chance of being hurt. Act like you don't know any other way to live.

There's one more thing that needs to be said.

Dogs will come and go from your life.

It's a simple, heartbreaking truth. You'll give your heart to each dog in your life and you'll watch them live out their story, puppyhood to passing. And, each passing will flatten you. You'll have to say goodbye to many dogs over the years. Each time, you'll vow never to go through that again; and, without fail, you'll fall in love with another dog.

Don't put your armor on. Don't walk away from the loving, fulfilling, joyous, life-enriching relationship with these animals because they will eventually leave you. Don't rob yourself of that joy because you're unwilling to feel the pain. You'll feel the pain anyway.

Give your heart. Get lost in those deep soulful eyes, stroke that soft fur, let those little puppy teeth nip at your fingers. Open your soul to that next journey. It fills you up more than it empties you, even at the end.

Be generous, be kind to them.

When it's their time to rest forever, send them off with a kiss and a whisper. *"Thank you. Thank you for choosing me. Thank you for all the kisses and love and cuddles and joy. I'm so grateful for the time we shared. Thank you."*

And, let them go. Forgive them for not living longer.

Thank them for marking your soul with their presence.

Forgive yourself for wanting to make them stay with you forever.

And, let them go.

They'll find you again. It's what they do. I promise.

Life Lesson Challenges
- What lessons have you learned from dogs, cats, or other pets in your life?
- How could you live your life with more *live for the moment* mentality?
- What would change in your life if you loved unconditionally, especially yourself?
- If you're not a pet owner, how do the above lessons resonate for you?

LIFE LESSON 41

I Wish I Knew About the Inherent Duality of our Human Existence

This is a concept that continues to challenge and electrify me. You may have heard this concept expressed other ways, such as the *'tyranny of or'*, meaning that only binary choices are available to us. Yes *or* no. Hot *or* cold. Up *or* down. When I surrendered to the notion that I can be, do, love, think more than one thing at once, it was groundbreaking. I hadn't appreciated how much energy I was investing in trying to figure out which was the *right* choice. I didn't appreciate that I could hold two seemingly opposing ideas in my consciousness at once and be at peace. Like a dual-faucet sink, you can tinker with the flow rates, blending hot and cold water to find your optimal temperature. I can be both courageous and terrified while still moving towards my goal. I didn't have to banish fear to progress; in fact, sinking my energy into banishing the fears stops all momentum. I just had to accept fear's presence, hold onto my courage, and walk forward.

❦ ❦ ❦ ❦ ❦ ❦

Dear Lisa,

Your scientist training will impart a sense that the world can easily be demarcated into discrete categories. You will warm to the concept of binary thinking and, for most of your life, this will not necessarily impede your progress. You'll apply this dualistic thinking to external things like weather, schoolwork, or sports.

Not until you start down this journey of self-actualization will you really struggle with duality.

For example, once you decide to live the life of an entrepreneur, you'll climb into what I'll affectionately call the Dual-A-Coaster (i.e., the rollercoaster of duality). Your soul will be yanked from emotion to emotion as you *swing* from passion to fear to joy to crushing uncertainty to revelation to frustration. All perfectly normal for any entrepreneur and all very distressing to someone who believed that *real* entrepreneurs only feel passion. They don't feel fear or uncertainty, right?

You'll rationalize this binary belief by citing successful businesspeople, highlighting where their journey took them, not, *crucially*, where they started.

If I knew then what I now know, I'd invite you to accept the Dual-A-Coaster as necessary part of your journey and re-focus your attention on your goals.

You can be afraid and determined at the same time.

You can be hot *and* cold.

You can be tired *and* invigorated simultaneously.

Judging yourself as *less than* for experiencing this duality will only slow you down. Embrace all the wonderful complexity that is you and your experience in this world, no matter where you are in your journey.

Life Lesson Challenges

- How true is it that whatever choice or crossroads you're facing only has binary solution?
- How does duality show up in your life?
- If you've had success embracing duality, what lessons would you share with others, with your past self?

LIFE LESSON 42

I Wish I Knew How to Play Big

This lesson is related to Life Lesson #7 around showing up authentically and takes it one step further. This is my invitation to my younger self (and you!), to show up courageously in all your glorious authenticity, especially in the face of external criticism and naysayers.

🍍 🍍 🍍 🍍 🍍 🍍

Dear Lisa,

There will be people in your life who will try to keep you quiet, keep you in the corner, and keep you playing small. There will be men and women in your life who want nothing more than for you to sit still, keep quiet, and make their lives easy.

One day during grad school, you'll swing by the bookstore on your way to the lab. You have a well-developed sweet tooth and are craving gummy bears. As you queue up to pay for your snacks, you hear a male voice say *very* loudly, "A *moment on the lips, an eternity on the hips. Right, Lisa?*" The cashier and all of the customers within ear shot turn and stare at you. Shame will course through your body. Turning around, you realize the male voice belongs to a fellow grad student; the dude who has sat next to you for four months during a class and never spoken to you. Until that moment. Overwhelmed by shame and completely self-conscious, you put down the gummy bears and run of the store. By the time you've jogged the ten minutes to your lab, hot tears are coursing down your face. It's totally understandable that you react that way.

Sadly, that won't be the last time people give unsolicited advice. Your time in the corporate world will be marked by similar incidents.

Here are some other examples of what it sounds like when someone is trying to keep you down, as a result of their internal narrative:

- "Whoa, easy now, you're getting a head of yourself."
- "Slow down there, pump the brakes."
- "That's a lot of opinions for one young lady."
- "I'm not sure you understand what you're saying."
- "Are you sure that's the dress you want to wear?"

In most cases, it's not really worth figuring out why these people struggle with who you are and how you show up in the world. It all boils down to you being *you*.

Here's what I invite you to do instead:
- Laugh it off and move on.
- Tell them to mind their own business (or use 'f*ck off' for *really* persistent people).
- Be audacious.
- Enjoy dessert.
- Wear what makes you feel good.
- Share your opinion, openly and honestly.
- Sing when people tell you to keep quiet.
- Dance when people tell you to sit still.

When you show up fully, life changes. People are drawn to you. Ideas flood your brain. Joy persists. And slowly, surely those critical voices grow quiet.

We are all at different points in our journey and people in your life may not be ready or comfortable with the changes you're making in yours. They may instinctively try to dampen your enthusiasm to deflect their discomfort.

Don't let other people's discomfort control your destiny. Play big.

Life Lesson Challenges
- How are you playing small in your life, holding back thoughts or actions to avoid criticism?
- What stories are you telling yourself that keeps you playing small?
- What would it feel like to live your life more audaciously?
- What's one thing you can change about how you show up this week?

LIFE LESSON 43

I Wish I Knew How to Let Others Evolve in Their Own Time

This lesson goes hand-in-hand with the discussions around non-judgement and awareness. It also reminds me of the cliché my family used to use when someone was getting too bossy: *keep your own doorstep clean*. In other words, focus on your needs and your business. No need to come next door and start trying to tell your neighbors how to sweep their doorstep. The other crucial component of living this lesson – like so many others in this book – is compassion. Compassion for yourself for wanting to bring people along who aren't ready, and compassion for others as they navigate their journey.

🌵 🌵 🌵 🌵 🌵 🌵

Dear Lisa,

Building on our last lesson around playing big (Life Lesson #42), you will encounter many people that are not ready for the self-actualization. Or they may have different views of what that means. Or they may be wrestling with how best to get started.

You are on *your* journey: finding out who you really are and what you really want to do with your life.

When you finally hear that call and make your big leap (which you will), there will be moments when you look around and notice that people aren't keeping pace with you. They're there but they're not *there*.

And, this will frustrate you. A sense of uncertainty and even fear will creep into your mind. You worry. What if I end up here all self-actualized but completely alone?

In response to that worry, you lash out at people who are still trying to figure out this whole life purpose thing.

You see people making choices that you know (or that you *think* you know) are based on fear and not on a conscious choice. You'll want to shake them by their shoulders and rip the cards out of their hand.

C'est la vie, right? If people ask about your journey, share what feels right to share, but don't blame them if they're not ready. Don't try to drag them along. It'll hurt both of you.

Look. It's *their* journey. It's *their* dance. It's *their* hand of cards to play. Let them play it. Spend your energy to fuel your journey.

People have to make these decisions in their own time. Trying to force the issue will leave everyone depleted, frustrated, and bitter. Not fun.

This lesson goes both ways. Your journey may make someone in your life really uncomfortable. It might make more than one person in your life uncomfortable. Know that this discomfort is all about them and nothing to do with you. It'll be hard to see that sometimes. And, even harder to live it, when it means watching relationships slowly dissolve.

Everything has a life span. Let things wax and wane as they need to, as you need them to. Be compassionate with yourself for trying to bring them along with you. Have compassion for others as they negotiated the ups and downs of their own journey.

And, for heaven's sake, don't try to coach someone unless they ask you to. Don't confuse eagerness to use your coaching skills with dispensing helpful advice. Coaching is about guiding and supporting someone towards *their* agenda not yours.

The best way to help someone progress on their journey is to keep living yours, whole-heartedly.

Life Lesson Challenges
- Have you felt that people in your life are growing at a different pace to you? If so, how did that impact your life and relationship?
- What would change if you let people come and go from your life, without you trying to cling to them?

LIFE LESSON 44

I Wish I Knew How to Truly Practice Kindness

I can't present this lesson without mentioning his Holiness the Dalai Lama. A beacon for hope, compassion, and kindness to humankind, the words of the Dalai Lama have always brought me so much comfort. I really began to live this kindness mantra as I started to cultivate awareness of just how much judgement I was carrying around; judgement against myself and others. These days when I find myself in a situation where discomfort starts to rise and I feel the urge to judge myself or others, I ask myself, *"What is the kindest thing I can do right now?"* Without fail, an answer to that question presents itself. And, typically, it's not what my default response would be; it's typically an opportunity for growth. I invite you to try it. It certainly changed my life.

Dear Lisa,

I know that you are a person who strives to be giving and compassionate. I'm going to challenge to expand that instinct. I'm going to challenge you to be kind. To everyone.

Being nice to someone can be a cloaking device (Star Trek reference…nerd alert!), masking true feelings of envy, blame, frustration or defiance. You may be nice to people because it's polite, socially acceptable, and reflects your ability to adapt to situations. After all, being a chameleon is one of your superpowers. It may be in your self-interest to be nice; it may bring you someone or something you want.

Being *kind* is linked to your sense of personal ethics and values. You empathize with someone when you are kind; you are seeking to help that person more than you're trying to help yourself. Kindness is often more difficult to achieve than niceness. It requires more self-awareness, more consciousness, and an empathetic world-view.

Let me share an example. During the holidays, you'll work at Williams-Sonoma to help cover costs during grad school. It's really a dream job given the proximity to high-end kitchen gadgets and foodie cookbooks.

Working a retail job during the holiday season is not for the faint of heart, and you certainly encounter your share of angry, frustrated, stressed customers. Being *nice* to an agitated customer might involve smiling through clenched teeth, helping them as best you can, all while avoiding eye contact and fantasizing about evicting them dramatically from the store. *Take that you ungrateful sh*t*, you'll want to scream! This is certainly a normal and completely understandable reaction when faced with a disgruntled customer.

My challenge to you is to imagine what it would look and feel like to treat that same customer with *kindness*. Can you put yourself in their shoes? What is the kindness thing you could do for them? Maybe you smile genuinely, without clenched teeth. Maybe you make eye contact and listen to their story. Seek to understand their story without judgement.

Approaching life this way will alter your energy level during social interactions. The instinct to judgement when discomfort or frustration arises will largely dissipate; it won't disappear completely because you are, after all, human.

While you're practicing being kind to other people, extend that kindness to yourself. Ask yourself that same question: *what's the kindest thing I can do for myself, right now?*

Life Lesson Challenges
- How do you know when you're being *nice* but not *kind?* What's different about how you feel and act?
- When have you experienced niceness or kindness in the past few months?
- Which one *feels* better to you: niceness or kindness?
- What stops you from being *kind* to everyone you encounter?

LIFE LESSON 45

I Wish I Knew How to Surrender

These days, when I sense I'm gearing up to fight against my self-critical voices, I consciously pause. I journal, take a walk, listen to music, clean the house, jump on the bike trainer for a spin, meditate; any activity that removes my pre-frontal cortex from the situation and allows me to tap into my intuition and Higher Self. More often than not, clarity arrives in short order: I can see the next step. I can't see *all* the steps to my goal, but I can see the next one. Surrendering the need to crystal-ball the perceived *productivity* and allow the clarity to emerge has been a game-changer.

Dear Lisa,

This will be a tough lesson for you.

I feel like I say that every time; but, no, seriously, this one *is* a challenge.

The Webster's dictionary definition of *surrender* is, in part, to "cease resistance to an enemy or opponent." Note, this definition does not include the following words: losing, loser, giving up, weak, wussy, unable to cut it in life, and all the other things you typically associate with the concept of *surrendering*.

The part I like best in this definition is "cease resistance." In the context of your self-development, this is where the big magic lies.

Let's unpack this a little more.

Who is the enemy, when it comes to your inner growth and evolution? Yourself, right? Yes, but in more granular terms, the enemy is the *self-critical* aspect of you, that ego flavor that seeks to protect you at all costs.

So, what does ceasing your resistance to those self-critical inner voices, your *gremlins*, look like? Does that mean that they're gonna run your life? I know you're watching that scene play out in your head. It looks like a swarm of zombies rushing into your life, destroying your world and generally wreaking havoc.

No. It means the opposite, because gremlins *love* resistance. The more you resist, the more they grow in potency and volume. Resistance to a gremlin is validation that there's some fear or lack in your psyche that can be exploited. Pretty soon, you're spending your entire day trying to ignore the gremlin horde clamoring in your head.

I also want to clear something up: gremlins as not an evil force. They are created when you experience a shaming or traumatic event. In essence, they become our protectors in that moment. The gremlins whisper messages of self-protection in our ears: *stay small, don't risk it, don't be seen, stay quiet, you're not capable, you're not worthy*. These messages are not intended to injure you but to avoid feeling that pain or shame again. So, gremlins do serve a purpose in the immediate aftermath of that event. As you continue on your journey, the gremlin messages that used to serve you no longer do; in fact, they start to hold you back.

What if you let down your resistance, let the voices say what they will and simply listened? Not judged or tried to change the gremlins' message, not sought to prove the gremlin messages wrong.

What if, you laid down your self-righteous sword and just let the chips fall? Stop trying to control every single, bloody thing in your life. What if you sank back into the warm embrace of surrender and let the Universe figure out what's next for you?

Surrendering your drive to control outcomes, especially when gremlins are present, is *the* trust fail of all time. It's normal to feel fear and uncertainty.

I invite you to sink back, knowing that the Universal fabric is your safety net. Fall into it, let it catch you. Let it wrap you in warmth and certainty. Have a conversation with those gremlins. Thank them for protecting you and release them. Step out of the over-thinking, analysis-paralysis and let clarity reveal itself.

Because, trust me, the only certainty in life is that there will always be uncertainty. And, all you're doing by repeatedly hammering away at trying to control every little thing and trying to silence those gremlin voices, is exhausting yourself. Makes me tired just typing that.

Sink into *surrender*, trust the Universe will catch you, and that you'll see the signs when it's time to change directions.

Life Lesson Challenges

- Are you someone who feels the need to control outcomes, people's actions, or people's emotions?
- How does it feel to watch things turn out differently, when you've put so much energy into trying to dictate the outcome?
- What can you actually, really, 100% control in any situation? Be honest.

LIFE LESSON 46

I Wish I Knew How to Hold Myself Accountable

Accountability has become an essential part of my vocabulary and existence. I have always been a list-maker. My to-do lists are things of beauty. Categorized, color-coded and arranged chronologically. That doesn't necessarily mean that I am capable of holding myself accountable for my actions. It means I know what tasks I need to accomplish. They are different concepts. I have also found that accountability for tasks is the low hanging fruit. Accountability for my actions and emotional boundaries have been more challenging for me, especially when I'm acting out of alignment with my values. This is something I am constantly aware of and seeking to improve. I have a coach and an amazing tribe that help keep me accountable. I invite you to explore how accountability – or taking our current accountability to the next level – could benefit your life.

❧ ❧ ❧ ❧ ❧ ❧

Dear Lisa,

I know you are a responsible person. You take a lot of pride in planning out your activities and checking things off your to-do lists.

This goes beyond taking responsibility for the success or simple tasks; that's necessary, sure, and there's even more you can work on.

Start taking radical accountability for things you do that don't work out, hurt people, or go against your values.

Radical accountability is owning your story, your role in each speedbump and milestone, committing to learn from those experiences, and paying it forward. It's accountability taken to the next level.

The best example I can give you is an incident that will take place in Northern California, shortly after you move there from the East Coast. You are running low on money. You have applied for a few jobs but there's no guaranteed employment in sight. And you're drinking a lot more than is healthy for you (or anyone, really). One night, you are extremely drunk – it's difficult to walk—and you get into a physical altercation. You feel physically threatened and you fight back.

You have never been afraid of a fight, so you throw yourself into the fray. The police will show up. You will be arrested on felony assault charges. As the policeman folds you into the backseat of his cruiser, you have a panic attack. Claustrophobia – which you thought you'd beat years ago – will suffocate you, your hands restrained behind you, your face pressed sideways into the narrow backseat. You can't breathe and darkness starts to close in. You start screaming and kicking against the seat.

The rest of the next few hours will be a blur. You'll choke and sputter on the drive to the police station. You vaguely remember being fingerprinted and stripped of your belongings. You will wake up lying on the floor of a holding cell, blink confusedly, and then pass out again. You'll be out for an unknown length of time and wake up back in the bed at your rental cabin. You'll vaguely remember being released and driven back to the campground. Court paperwork lies on the floor by your crumpled jacket. The worst hangover you've ever felt is reverberating throughout your entire body. Your partner is curled up on the bed next to you. And you'll start crying.

You will appear at court a few days later and experience terror you didn't know was possible. You will shake so violently with fear that when the bailiff calls your name it's hard to stand.

The judge will ask you to be honest about what happened. You tell him what you remember. The alcohol dulled everything; the blackout leaves huge gaps in your memory. He tells you what the police reports says, and you will not be able to hold back tears. It feels like the world is holding its breath as the judge confers with the prosecutor; it is hard to hear because your heart is pounding so loudly in your chest. You know that they have the right to charge and imprison you. You know that a felony charge will end your life as you know it. In your mind, that felony record – a poor, drunk decision on the worst night your life – erases your doctorate, your job history, all your accomplishments, everything *good* in your life.

You are granted a reprieve. No charges are filed. You will let out a huge exhale.

Fate flipped a coin and you walk free.

While you may not have a felony record, you carry the shame of that arrest for the rest of your life. It will also change the way you view people carrying that record on their backs.

We're not different, we're the same. That could've been me, save for the flip of a coin.

We're all human, we all make mistakes. That doesn't mean that we can escape the consequences just because we're all trying to figure stuff out.

Will this accountability practice be uncomfortable? You betcha.

Is this necessary? Yes. Absolutely.

Why? Because not taking responsibility for your actions or decisions erodes your soul. It's not an *inconvenience*. It literally starts to chip away at your existential well-being. This is serious stuff.

Here's the short version of how to take radical accountability:
1. Apologize, sincerely.
2. Describe what you did, said and felt. This is owning your story.
3. Share how you'll make it right or make amends.
4. Pay it forward by sharing these experiences with others.

This doesn't just apply to other people. This applies to you, yourself. Be accountable for choices you make that hurt *you*.

Apologize and find a way to make amends. And, as always, practice self-compassion. You did the best you could with where you were in your life.

Life Lesson Challenges
*   Where in your life are you avoiding taking accountability?
*   Where or when is accountability easier to achieve?
*   How do you feel when you take accountability? What is the response from people in your life?
*   What would owning your story look like for you? What gets in the way?

LIFE LESSON 47

I Wish I Knew How to Start before I Was Ready

The life of an entrepreneur is not for everyone. Some days, I wonder if it's right for me! This lesson revolutionized how I approach business and life decisions. If I had waited until I was *ready* to walk away from a lucrative job to be self-employed you would not likely be reading this book. I'm writing this book and I'm still not 100% sure I'm ready to be a published author. There have certainly been moments in my life when that uncertainty and crystal-balling (see Life Lesson 45 on *Surrendering*) have stopped me in my tracks.

Dear Lisa,

When you're contemplating big changes, you'll invariably ask yourself, *"Am I ready for this?"*

Honestly, when is the answer to that question ever 100%? We can always conjure up worst case scenarios and disastrous outcomes.

For example, I'll ask you: are you ready to quit a high paying job, with excellent benefits, to start a bakery business which may deplete your savings, alienate your family, then crash and burn so bad they'll practically write a special editorial warning young people against these type of foolhardy schemes in the local paper? Honestly, that's pretty close to a 90% 'yes'.

The point is, you'll never (or very, very, very rarely) feel 100% up for anything new, except *perhaps* trying a new flavor of ice cream.

Let's go back to that bakery business. It's been a dream of yours for years. The desire to pivot from your marketing career to become a professional baker will eventually outweigh your arguments against it.

So, yes, you start the bakery business. For almost a year, you are elbow deep in flour and butter. You navigate all the necessary paperwork – even though you have no idea how to do it. You are determined to see this bakery come to life. At first, it's a home bakery business. Every surface in your tiny rental house is covered in pies, cakes, cookies, and breads; much to the delight of your partner and dogs!

You work diligently, building the plane as you fly it, answering questions from the health department, creating recipes, sourcing ingredients. And then, one Sunday morning, you'll be standing under a tent behind a table laden with your baked goods, a big banner proudly proclaiming that your bakery business is now open for business. If you'd waited until you knew exactly how everything would turn out, what it would require of you, it's doubtful if you would have seen this dream come true.

But you did it. Because you just f-ing did it.

So, don't wait for the 100%. Maybe this time it's not a bakery. Make those dreams a reality. You did it before, you can do it.

When you have a dream – and you'll have many – start it. Do it. Jump in.

Otherwise, you trade bliss for disappointment, over and over.

Life Lesson Challenges
- What goals have you accomplished, even though you started before you felt ready?
- Where and how in your life are you waiting for that 100% *Yes* before acting?
- What would change in your life, if you started *before* you were ready?
- How would it feel to build the plane as you fly it, as you pursue your work and your dreams?

LIFE LESSON 48

I Wish I Knew How to Stop Apologizing for *Everything*

There is always a time and place for apologies. Make no mistake, when I upset someone (intentionally or unintentionally), I apologize. When I accidentally run over someone's foot with a shopping cart, because I'm staring at a yummy pile of avocados, I apologize. When I bump into someone in a crowded airport, apologize. You get my point. This lesson is about *compulsive* apologizing. Apologizing for being *me*. For breathing. This constant need to apologize, in my opinion, is tied to waning self-esteem or self-identity. It's not really saying sorry, its saying, *please don't get mad, don't alienate me, I don't want to be excluded from this tribe*. That's a horse of a different color. This compulsion can still sneak up on me. If I'm deep in victim mode or disconnected from my sense of self, and just starting to process that awareness, I may not realize it until I catch onto the fact that I'm starting all my sentences with, "I'm sorry." Once I realized how often I was saying, "Sorry," instead of what I really felt, I made a conscious effort to change my language and reframe that impulse. Words have power, not just for others but for us, too.

🌵 🌵 🌵 🌵 🌵 🌵

Dear Lisa,

As a caring, kind person you'll start apologizing out of politeness and social good graces. Then, you'll find the word slipping out of your mouth with every interaction.

Sorry, I made eye contact.

Sorry, I didn't put your glass in the right spot on your desk.

Sorry, I didn't put your mail in the right inbox.

Sorry, I didn't leave a voicemail.

Sorry, I didn't make the right choice for you.

It will become a compulsion, a tic that you can't control. Every time you ask for this forgiveness, it erodes your confidence and self-esteem.

This apologizing really boils down to constantly feeling like you're not measuring up to someone's expectations (or your own expectations). Often times, you will be seeking comfort and reassurance when this compulsion shows up. By apologizing, you are inviting the other person to forgive you for your perceived underperformance.

It comes down to feeling *less than*.

You are not alone in feeling this way. It's totally understandable given what you are facing and your life story up until that point.

Here's my invitation for you: when you feel the instinct to say *I'm sorry*, take a few breaths, and start the sentence with, "*Thank you.*"

"*Thank you for waiting,*" instead of, "*Sorry I'm late.*"

"*Thank you for understanding,*" instead of, "*Sorry I let you down.*"

"*Thank you for listening,*" instead of, "*Sorry I talk so much.*"

"*Thank you for this meeting,*" instead of "*Sorry to take up your time.*"

"*Thank you for your attention,*" instead of, "*Sorry to bother you.*"

Constantly seeking approval is like living in quicksand. Every apology pulls you down a little further into the muck (in this case, the victim energy).

There's nothing wrong with reassurance but when you (or anyone) gets stuck in that victim energy, it becomes your world. It's hard to see opportunities or have the energy to pursue them. When you stop constantly cutting yourself down with this apologizing you will notice a lightening of spirit. You will inch your way out of the muck.

Try pairing this new habit with other learning in this book - like self-love and self-compassion - and you will notice a distinct shift in your energy.

Life Lesson Challenges

- Do you ever catch yourself apologizing over and over again when there really isn't a specific incident or accident?
- What would shift in your mindset and life if you found a way to stop apologizing?
- Try replacing "I'm sorry," with, "Thank you." How does this change your experience? What happens?

LIFE LESSON 49

I Wish I Knew That Not Everyone is Gonna Get Me. And That's Okay.

A lot of us outgrow this need to be accepted and liked in our late teens. When we make the transition to adulthood, our ego-driven life choices often dispel this issue. For me, it never really disappeared. There were years when it wasn't as evident, but it was always a faint refrain in the background of my life. A series of life challenges, beginning with my divorce and ending with that arrest in Northern California, brought me face to face with this life lesson repeatedly. Changing who you are, what you believe, or how you act to gain someone's approval is a losing proposition.

🌵 🌵 🌵 🌵 🌵 🌵

Dear Lisa,

Wanting to be liked by everyone in your life is a slippery slope.

At different times in your life, you'll try to change who you are and how you act to make people happy, to feel accepted.

Sometimes, they'll be little things: the food you eat or the music you listen to.

Other times, you'll try to morph fundamental values and pieces of your soul.

You'll chip away at pieces of who you are – how to treat people, how you treat yourself, how you do business, how you spend money – in order to fit in with new crowds and new people. This façade may seem harmless in the short term, but your willingness to compromise these parts of yourself will rip up the anchor on your life.

You'll feel aimless, cut adrift from self-identity for several years, bouncing between ideologies and groups. I think this is probably normal for that time in people's life: questioning who you are and where you're going.

This will all come to a head when you're standing by a moving van, your belongings scattered on the sidewalk, with a summer sky threatening rain in Boston.

You'll realize that 90% of the stuff you own, you bought because someone else in your life wanted it, or you thought you should buy it to fit in. You'll stand there, essentially paralyzed, trying to decide which disparate piece of your life up to this point, to leave behind. People walk by on the sidewalk, stepping around your bookcases, stacks of pillows, and boxes of random kitchen tools. You'll shake your head because you can't quite believe that you own any of these things. It's like you're helping someone else move; that's how unconnected you'll feel from everything.

Suddenly something cracks open in your psyche at the thought of stacking all of this stuff into the moving van (which you will shortly drive overnight all the way to North Carolina).

Anger will swell up in you and you'll start yanking stuff out of the moving van. Clothes, curtains, dishes, DVDs. Stuff. More and more stuff that you don't love or want. Tangible connections with people that you want to disconnect from your life. Memories that you've been carting around because jettisoning them felt like a betrayal. It will all come flooding out on that sidewalk.

A few hours later, your tiny studio apartment is cleared out and your absurdly large twenty-seven-foot moving van will be barely half full.

The parking cop has stopped by twice to check your permit for parking the van.

This entire scene is a microcosm of your life and social relationships for the past decade: clinging to things that didn't serve you, despite obvious opportunities to get rid of it, and severe penalties for failing to follow the *rules*.

The sidewalk is cluttered with boxes, furniture, and random items.

Rummaging in a box, you'll grab a handful of index cards and a Sharpie. (Side note: never go anywhere without a sharpie. Trust me.)

You start making index cards signs saying: Free. Free. Free. Free.

Signs go up on all the sidewalk stuff. People will appear out of doorways and cabs. Within ten minutes, all that literal and figurative baggage will be gone. The sense of freedom will be profound.

It'll be a lesson that you won't learn completely that day.

There'll still be moments when you second-guess if you're

enough for someone or some situation. You'll find yourself reverting into your chameleon ways. Changing your colors to blend in, trying to make sure you didn't stand out in a *bad* way.

Listen, what you have, and who you are, is special. There's no one like you. There won't be anyone like you.

If people don't get you, like you, love you, accept you, just be okay with it. Let it go. Let your people, your tribe find you.

If people don't pick up what you're puttin' down, fair enough. So be it.

You have too much to offer the world *just as you are* to diminish that light.

Please, give the people what they really want: *you*.

Life Lesson Challenges
- When in your life have you blunted your personality, beliefs, values, in order to feel accepted by a person or group?
- What was the result of this desire to be accepted or to fit in?
- How would it feel to show up fully, even if that means losing relationships?
- What is the cost of staying hidden versus showing up?

LIFE LESSON 50

I Wish I Knew That My Life Journey Was Going to Be More Like an Ironman Than a 5K

Before my tumor-removal surgery, I suffered a massive pulmonary embolism and was rushed to the hospital. I was lucky to receive timely intervention and spent the next few days recovering in the cardiac intensive care unit. When you're a patient, you have a lot of time to think. I used that time to contemplate how I wanted my life to be different. I knew that I didn't want to be back there anytime soon. More than anything I felt this intense pull toward running. I just wanted to tie on some sneakers and run à la Forrest Gump. I wanted to feel the wind and sun on my face, my feet pounding over packed dirt, my legs straining against the pace. Thanks to the great care I received, I was soon released and made a promise to myself that I would keep fitness at the forefront of my various hobbies. Some might say I've gone a bit overboard with that promise, as I've spent the last thirteen years participating in triathlon, including a full-length IRONMAN® and a sprinkling of Half-IRONMAN® races. My participation in triathlon has provided incredible opportunities for self-discovery and growth. Not to mention some really cool t-shirts.

* * * * * *

Dear Lisa,

You have always loved sports – both spectating and participating.

In a few years, you will be introduced to triathlon. Despite some initial skepticism, you will fall in love with the sport. You will compete in dozens of races, including a full-length IRONMAN®.

You will swim 2.4 miles, bike 112 miles, run a marathon and cross the finish line in a state of pure and complete euphoria. Sounds like a great way to spend a Sunday, right?

Plus, there's a t-shirt, bragging rights and a medal.

Your relationship with triathlon will evolve over time; the mileage on your body will take a toll. The life lessons you have learned as a result will serve you well within and outside the sport.

I bring this up because your life is a hell of lot more like an IRONMAN® triathlon than a road race. You're not just gonna lace up your existential sneakers and run on a well-paced road for a few miles, surrounded by orderly crowds of fellow runners.

You will face challenges on multiple fronts. You will face cancer. You will navigate divorce. You will get hurt and face lengthy physical recovery.

I tell you this not to dull your spirit but to give you a clearer picture of what to expect.

Don't expect smooth pavement for your entire journey.

Expect to make adjustments mid-journey, look for the potholes and speed bumps.

Accept them, learn from them, and move on.

(And, it doesn't mean you're attracting these challenges to you no matter what people tell you.)

It just means you're experiencing *life*, in all its dimensions.

Life Lesson Challenges
- How would viewing life as multi-sport adventure rather than a straight course change your experience? How would it change?
- How successful are you at navigating the obstacles life throws at you?
- What does wishing life's road was *smoother* actually cost you?

LIFE LESSON 51

I Wish I Knew How to Become
My Biggest Fan

I n 2019, women are more likely to experience shame about how they look than anything else. And, I am no different. Up until a few months ago, I struggled mightily with self-body shaming. I was never subjected to external shaming or bullying (or at least, they didn't do this to my face). I simply could not accept that my body was changing as I aged and that all my *tricks* to lose weight weren't working because the rules of the game were also changing. I also believe that all this body shame led to numbing with food, which led to more weight gain, which fed the shame. This self-perpetuating cycle really spun out of control over the past few years, exacerbated by the fact that I have been in peri-menopause since my cancer diagnosis nearly fifteen years ago. All that to say, becoming my biggest fan, especially when it came to my appearance, seemed like a big ask. Through supportive coaching, I began to break free of the self-judgement and shame, moving towards self-acceptance. I struggle with this on certain days when my energetic boundaries are more porous than normal, thanks to my influencers being off (e.g., sick, tired, hungry, traveling). The gift of being able to look in the mirror and love what's looking back at me unconditionally is priceless. I wholeheartedly wish I could pass that gift onto every woman struggling to be her biggest fan.

Dear Lisa,

You'll rarely walk through the world without hearing comments about how to *improve* your appearance.

Lose weight, gain weight, longer hair, shorter hair, clearer skin, more makeup, less makeup, dress this way, wear this, don't wear this. Everyone will have an opinion. Including yourself and your gremlins.

Your innate desire to be accepted and loved (a desire we all have) will extend to your appearance. For several disastrous months, you'll starve yourself to finally achieve that elusive allure. You'll be emotionally vulnerable after a divorce and decide that you'll control the only thing you can actually control—your weight, your diet, your exercise.

It'll start subtlety enough. Restrict a few calories here, run a few extra miles. After ten months of this mentality, you'll have lost 60 pounds, while gaining muscle. You'll be teetering on the edge of a dangerous situation.

This will also be the only time in your life when complete strangers – men and women – will walk up and compliment you. *You look amazing. Great body. Love your outfit.* So, where's the impetus to change? Why let yourself be healthy or eat? Why question what you're doing when *this* is the reaction?

Eventually, the decision will be taken out of your control because you'll get hurt, literally. A few broken bones, nothing serious.

During your rehabilitation, other people begin making food choices for you. I mean, you're in a wheelchair, right? You aren't hunkered down in your apartment with an empty fridge or working out in the gym all alone. People around you – your family and loved ones – care for you. This will be challenging, as you're pretty sure you've never needed anyone to do anything for you, pretty much since birth. Your independent spirit is well-developed. Having to ask for help, to have others take care of you will really challenge your self-confidence (see Life Lesson #20).

And, you're in the South. Did I not mention this? The home of fried food, homestyle cooking, and world-class barbeque. (Two words: *Cajun fries*.)

Suffice to say, you start to re-stablish your relationship with food. And, if you're honest, it's wonderful. It will be freeing to not constantly scrutinize every morsel, weighing the food you consume against how much exercise you'll need to work it off.

As you age, your weight will naturally increase (metabolism slows with age). Once again, those voices will start ratcheting up in your head: *too fat, too gross, too heavy, too ugly*. You'll start fighting with the urge to go back to that time when you were complimented by everyone on how you looked. Your rationale: that would ensure that you were accepted and loved by the ones closest to you.

Experts will tell you that the origin of these compulsions trace back to low self-esteem and a feeling of being unlovable.

There isn't a quick fix; this is a long slog for you. It can be distilled down to avoiding comparison and cultivating a sense of deep worthiness.

Hang in there. Do the work. Talk to the people you need to talk to.

But, most of all, and this is extremely important, believe your loved ones when they say, "*I love you just the way you are.*" Accepting yourself as you are, will lift a psychic burden that you've been carrying for decades. Tasks that used to be emotionally-fraught, like putting on shorts and a t-shirt to run a few errands with your partner, will be an afterthought and, even pleasurable.

If people leave your life because of the way you look, let them go (or, preferably, hit the eject button yourself).

There's nothing about your body or looks that needs to be changed. Every freckle, every wrinkle, every curve is right where it needs to be.

Become your biggest fan. Rave about yourself to you.

Love yourself intensely.

Life Lesson Challenges
- What is your relationship to your body image? Have you struggled with it?
- How has your struggle impacted your relationships? Why, or why not?
- What changes, if any, would happen if you worked to improve your body image?

LIFE LESSON 52

I Wish I Knew How to Be the Author of My Own Life Story

Story plays such a critical role in our lives. Our brains are hard-wired for narrative. We crave completion of the arc: beginning, middle, and end. In the absence of clear data, we tend to fill in the missing pieces with assumptions, beliefs and past experiences. Sometimes those assumptions support us; sometimes they break us down. I can't tell you what to believe or assume about your journey. I will invite you to own the story you've lived to this point, identify the lessons, integrate the knowledge, and write your own life story. (See Life Lesson #46 on accountability for even more inspiration.) There's no one more qualified to be the author of your life story and the captain of your ship, than you.

Dear Lisa,

There is a tipping point in your journey when you cast off passivity and jump into the driver's seat. Up until that point, you will often feel at the mercy of the world. You will feel buffeted by the winds of fate, powerless to chart your own course.

During this time of your life, your story owns you. You'll carefully edit your resume, deleting those times when you'll question whether or not you're succeeding: your arrest, your unemployment, your bouts of depression, all the years you struggled to make ends meet financially. You'll let self-induced shame and comparanoia rule your decisions.

When you decide to start owning your story, you'll dedicate time to figure out what your calling is. You'll quit jobs, travel across the country, consult experts, hire coaches, and read dozens of books. You'll listen to hundreds of hours of podcasts. You'll enroll in training programs. You'll attend workshops and retreats.

You'll become a huge consumer of information, sorting through these for ideas and concepts that resonate deeply with you. You'll start meditating every day, at least once a day. You'll cry. A lot. You'll walk away from toxic relationships. You'll start painting and writing and sketching.

You'll start allowing those intuitive hits to land, to become goals and strategies, guiding you towards a new life.

I invite you to believe that you can't make a mistake, that every decision you made was the best you could do, given what you were facing with the time. Retrospective self-blame and self-flagellation won't change anything and only holds you back.

I invite you to own the entire *tapestry* of your life. Every event, relationship, and choice contributed to the richness of your life.

Some of us start living their story very early in life. Others – like you – uncover their narrative slowly, chipping away at the armor encasing their true Self, bit by bit. They may arrive at a point where nothing in their life seems to work. They may feel a tug towards a life that is new to them. They hear a small, quiet voice saying, *you're meant for something more, there's more to life than this*. They may wake up one day and decide to stop tolerating and rationalizing away their life.

In fact, you'll devote your coaching practice to helping others envision, create, and live their story, rather than standing outside their story and hustling for worthiness or belonging. You'll know, first hand, how changing your narrative can powerfully transform your life.

We all have stories we want to live.

My invitation to you is to start owning your story *now*.

Grab the tiller.

Be the author of your fate, the captain of your ship, the architect of your future.

Own your story and write the next chapter of *your* life.

Life Lesson Challenges
- What would it feel like to own your story, to *really* own your journey?
- What chapters of your life story do you avoid owning? Why?
- What would change in your life, if you truly owned your life story?
- So, if you're the author of your life story, what do you want the next chapter of your life to be?

CONCLUSION

We Only Get One Life

Flipping back through these pages, it feels like the dream trip of a lifetime is coming to an end.

You know that feeling, right? You're packing up your things, shaking sand out of your flip-flops, stuffing all the little bits of beauty you found into the nooks and crannies of your suitcase.

That's what this feels like to me. There's a lump in my throat. Even though I know I'm going to back to my *real* life when this book is finished, there's a certain magic I'm leaving behind.

And that magic is in the gathering of you and me: the gathering of our souls, in this paper and ink world, through pain, heartache, searching, joy, bliss, and passion. Magic was in everything you and I experienced.

I wanted to pull you in, dear reader, keep you safe, and still push you to the edge of the cliff so that you might see how far the horizon of your potential stretches.

And it stretches so far. These days, I can't tell where the ocean ends, and the horizon begins.

And, maybe that's the point, in the end.

I wanted to find the perfect way to end this book – the prose, the imagery, or the quote that would encapsulate how I feel looking back at this part of my journey. Eventually, I realized that I won't be able to do it. I can't. Only in combination, in synergy, can this experience be described. Only with both of our voices, memories, art, and laughter will a full picture emerge. Because this book, this *experience,* wasn't created in a vacuum. You, my beloved reader, are an essential element.

So, I'll keep packing my suitcase, taking one last look around the dream we've co-created here, knowing that every time I look through these pages I'll be transported right back here again.

I know you'll be making some of this magic in your real life, your life outside this book.

You might think that mountain is too high to climb. You might think you're not capable or not *really* ready.

The truth is, you can do anything. Especially if that *anything* means following your heart and filling it with love, passion, joy and abundance.

You can do anything, think anything, feel anything, love anything with *your* life. Your one, precious life.

I see you thinking about what that would feel like.

You're already sitting a little taller.

You're already glowing a little brighter.

A LOVE LETTER TO STRUGGLE

Dear Struggle,

I've been thinking about you a lot lately. These past weeks you've been ever present. The image that keeps coming to mind is that painting (ya' know, the one from *Good Will Hunting*?): a guy in rain slicks, rowing his boat into a storm, back hunched against the wind and rain, the boat's nose starting to climb a wave capped in angry foam. That's what these last few months have felt like. Constantly pulling and straining against the oars, trying to make progress in spite of the powerful waves crashing against our prow.

I know now who is rowing the boat. I thought it was Fate or Destiny or the Universe. I was wrong.

It's a woman.

A brave, selfless woman who sits there, day in and day out, gripping the rough wood, muscling through the peaks and valleys. Head down. Heart sick. Hands rubbed raw, but resolute.

She must feel her hands bleeding and torn. She must feel the unbearable ache in her shoulders and back.

She must want to give up.

But, she's not alone in her boat. She has with her all that she holds dear. And, even though her family pleads and begs him to stop – *take a break, let us take a turn, heal your hands, care for yourself* – she does not, *cannot* acquiesce. As much as she may want to, she can't let anyone take a turn at the helm. If she did and the boat capsized it would be a loss too great to bear. But, it's more than that. She believes deep, deep down that this burden is hers to bear. That she *can* bear it. That, yes, her hands will bleed; her back will ache; her faith may waver. And all the pleading and entreating to rest, to share the burden, to slow down – these only *weaken* her resolve, not strengthen it. If she can just keep rowing, she knows she'll reach that distant shore (the land of Hope and Joy). Even if, in those darkest hours, land is hard to see, she cannot, will not, stop striving. She must keep rowing. She must to keep her world afloat.

I know this now because I, today, realized I'm in the boat, too. I thought I was on the shore, watching this woman fight against you, Struggle, from afar. I thought I was banned from the boat, that no one heard my cries, my worry, my frantic efforts to relieve this woman's burden. But I've been in the boat the whole time.

In fact, our whole, tough, kooky little family is together on that boat as you toss us around, Struggle, as you seek to force us back to that safe shore.

And though all I can see is storm-darkened clouds and angry rain lashing against my face, even though fear and anxiety and desperation sometimes tear at my heart: I know one thing to be true. I'd rather be in that boat than anywhere else.

So, you keep rowing, my love.

If we take on water, I'll bail it out.

If you get weak or thirsty, I'll be there.

But keep rowing, keep doing what you *need* to do.

Our family is here – we're with you and we'll keep our faith with (and in) you, no matter how bad the storm may seem. I have my job to do, too – I am first mate, after all – I have my own burdens to bear. And, I'm up for that.

I'm all in.

So, thank you Struggle. Thank you for showing me where I want to be.

Thank you for giving me the chance to realize that I'm in a boat and that I *want* to go along for the ride.

I love you, Struggle, and I'm forever grateful.

ADDITIONAL RESOURCES

Here are a few books and resources that I've really benefitted from throughout my journey. If I feel the need for inspiration or clarity, I often go back to these books for a quick read.

This is just a partial list to get you started. Amazing books and resources are released every day. I encourage you to visit your library or favorite bookstore to discover even more incredible works.

Books

Brown, Brené. *Daring Greatly: How the Courage to Be Vulnerable Transforms the Way We Live, Love, Parent and Lead*. Random House, 2012. ISBN 9781592408412

Brown, Brené. *Dare to Lead: Bold Work. Tough Conversations. Whole Hearts*. Random House, 2018. ISBN 9780399592522

Brown, Brené. *Rising Strong*. Random House, 2015. ISBN 9780091955038

Brown, Brené. *The Gifts of Imperfection: Let Go of Who You Think You're Supposed to Be and Embrace Who You Are*. Hazelden Publishing, 2010. ISBN 9781592859894

Campbell, Joseph. *The Hero with A Thousand Faces*. New World Library, 2008. ISBN 9781577315933

Coelho, Paulo. *The Alchemist*. HarperCollins, 1988. ISBN 9780062315007

Dispenza, Joe. *Becoming Supernatural: How Common People Are Doing the Uncommon*. Hay House, 2017. ISBN 9781401953119

Keller, Gary (with Jay Papasan). *The ONE Thing: The Simple Truth Behind Extraordinary Results*. Bard Press. 2012. ISBN 9781885167774

Hill, Napoleon. Think and Grow Rich. Sound Wisdom (original 1937 first edition), 2016. ISBN 9781937879501.

Pressfield, Steven. *The War of Art: Break Through the Blocks and Win Your Inner Creative Battles*. Black Irish Entertainment, LLC., 2010. ISBN 9781936891023

Schneider, Bruce D. *Uncovering the Life of Your Dreams: An Enlightening Story*. John Wiley & Sons, 2018. ISBN 9781119469094

Sincero, Jen. *You Are A Badass at Making Money*. Viking, 2017. ISBN 9780735222977.

Tolle, Eckhart. *A New Earth: Awakening Your Life's Purpose*. Penguin Books, 2005. ISBN 9780452289963

Twist, Lynne. *The Soul of Money: Transforming Your Relationship with Money and Life*. W.W. Norton & Company, 2017. ISBN 9780393353976.

FREE BONUS WORKBOOK!

Hey there! How did you like the book?

Did you see my invitation at the beginning? No?

Who can blame you! I'm so impatient when I start a new book, I practically rip off the cover.

Here's the free workbook I mentioned:

I've created a free, downloadable companion workbook that guides you through each of these fifty-two life lessons so that you can create your own version of *Sh*t I Wish I Knew Yesterday*! Cool, right? I think so, too!

Head on over to siwiky-book.com/workbook to download your workbook.

Don't stop there: share the workbook with your friends, family, Facebook group, book club!

We all have a story to tell and I hope this workbook helps you realize how extraordinary you are!

I'm creating a virtual community to support everyone in sharing their stories, insights, and learnings.

A huge *thank you* to my readers and fans for all your support.

I can't wait to hear all about you and your life story!

xoxox

Lisa

ABOUT THE AUTHOR

Lisa Marie Nelson, PhD, ACC, CPC, ELI-MP

I n 2005 Lisa received her doctorate in Pathology from the University of North Carolina in Chapel Hill School of Medicine. Her doctoral research focused on the development of thermally stable, oral prodrugs to treat African trypanosomiasis (also known as African Sleeping Sickness).

After graduate school, Lisa relocated to the Boston area to begin a career in the biotech industry where, as a scientist, she co-authored several peer-reviewed publications and was listed on an issued US patent.

She's spent the last 15 years working within the biotech/pharma sector in a variety of roles, spanning multiple US companies. Lisa continues to contribute her highly valued and unique blend of science, creativity, leadership, and strategic vision to the important work of delivering new life-saving medicines to patients.

During a sabbatical from her biotech/biopharma career, Lisa trained at the Institute for Professional Excellence in Coaching (iPEC). She is a Certified Professional Coach (CPC), an Energy Leadership Index Master Practitioner (ELI-MP), and a certified Cor.E dynamic transition coach.

Following this certification, Lisa obtained her Associate Credential Coach (ACC) from the International Coaching Federation (ICF) in 2019, reflecting her remarkable commitment to coaching clients. She is also an IRONMAN® University Certified Coach and works with first-time triathletes determined to achieve their dream of completing an IRONMAN® race.

When not working, writing or coaching, Lisa can be found swimming, biking, running, and playing east of San Francisco with her partner and two (very spoiled) rescue dogs: Kona and Anela.

Connect with Lisa
siwiky-book@gmail.com // siwiky-book.com

ACKNOWLEDGEMENTS

To the team at Capucia Publishing: Christine, Carrie, Simon, Penny, Jean, and so many others. Thank you for helping my dreams come true. There is no other group that does what you do – the professional know-how, the joy, and the passion. I'm forever grateful for the chance to work with this dream team.

To my amazing coaches and tribe: Stacy Hartmann, everyone in the Society for Soulful Empire Builders, my beloved Truth Tears & Truth Bitchslaps group. Thank you for holding space for me during this journey, for your love, support, and (of course) the truth bitchslaps. *Seagull!*

Melissa Potter, Shanon Altig, and Missy McCracken, thank you for your peerless review (see what I did there?). I am so grateful for the gift of your feedback, incredible encouragement, guidance, and friendships. You helped me take a sh*tty first draft and turn it into a book that I am so incredibly proud of. Thank you!

To my siblings and their families: Thank you for always being there throughout my life journey. And for the amazing group text exchanges. You guys are the best.

To my niece and nephews: I hope you don't get in trouble for reading a book with curse words in it (I won't tell). I know I don't see all of you as much as I would like. Know that Aunt Lisa loves you very much and is always here for you, whatever you may need. And, yes, you have to wait until you're eighteen years old to get a tattoo.

To my parents: Norman and Pammula. You have sacrificed everything for us, for me, to create the life we dreamed of (no matter how crazy it seemed!). I am so proud to be your daughter. Words fail me. Thank you for your unconditional love and guidance. And for passing on your obsession with great coffee.

To Kona and Jordan: thanks for being the best pups anyone could ask for. Yes, you're in the acknowledgments, even if you can't read. And even if you hog the bed.

To Chad: You are the love of my life, my moon and my stars. My everything. Thank you for always believing in me. Thank you for being my partner in life and love. You are the bravest, strongest, most remarkable person I will ever know. I can't wait to see where our adventures take us.